PAYING THE PRICE

A Life in Football … and Beyond

EARNEL DURDEN

For more information contact:
Earnel Durden

Hardcover ISBN: 978-0-692-62504-0
eBook ISBN: 978-0-692-62503-3

Text design by Dotti Albertine

CONTENTS

CONTENTS

CHAPTER ONE

The Way Things Are
Isn't the Way Things Were

I **have been blessed** with a long memory. It's a good thing, too, because I've had a lot to keep track of over the last seventy-some years. Not only have I had more than my share of adventures in my personal life, I've also had a front-row seat for some of the greatest social and cultural upheavals of the 20th Century. In my own way, I've even taken part. Looking back, I am very thankful for my vivid memories from these events, which have allowed me to relive parts of my life as if they had happened just this morning.

I was only three years old when we left my birthplace, Jefferson, Texas. Apparently, that was old enough to have formed some indelible impressions. I remember that my father was a logger, driving what we called in those days a "puckwood truck." Essentially, it is a logging truck designed to carry the shorter logs of the "pulpwood" used to make paper products. But as I've grown older, I've come to wonder if that was his only occupation.

No one has ever confirmed it for me, but I've often suspected that my father may have been involved in selling liquor during the last days of Prohibition. On more than one occasion, he would bring home large, opaque containers. I remember the parties he would throw on the weekends for his friends and how the alcohol always seemed to be plentiful, even though large parts of the state would remain dry even after Prohibition ended.

Additionally, as my mother has indicated over the years, we were doing quite well financially—at least until the day when my mother, older brother, and I all came down with terrible colds. My mother went out to get some medication for us and, while she was gone, my older brother decided that he was going to be adult by smoking a cigarette. Unfortunately, his attempt at smoking was met with immediate consequences; he wound up burning down the house.

No one was hurt, but I realize now that losing the house must have been a huge blow to our finances at the time. But we weren't the only family experiencing some upheaval. The United States's entry into World War II changed everything, as war often does. I was too young to understand what was going on in the larger world; I only knew what was happening at my house—except that house was now gone. So, my parents were faced with finding us a new home.

There were good jobs available in military defense plants, which were cropping up all over the West Coast. When my father found work at a plant in San Pedro—a seaside community just south of Los Angeles—we said goodbye to Texas.

My father went ahead of us to get started at work, sending for us when he was ready. San Pedro had a deep harbor that hosted a number of Navy battleships, and it was an important part of the war effort. He was hardly the only person to head to the West Coast for this reason. In fact, the period of time between the onset of WWII and 1970 is often called "The Second Great Migration." The first, smaller migration was the movement of Black Americans from the rural South to Northern urban centers in 1910 to 1930.

It was the war that spurred one of the largest movements of Black Americans in the nation's history. Thousands of men, women, and children headed West in search of better jobs and opportunities than the low-paying trades that were available to African Americans in the South. Eventually, this mass movement would change the American racial landscape, as well as the makeup of cities like Los Angeles. Before the war, LA had a Black population of only 63,700. By 1970, there were more than 763,000 African Americans who called the city home.

It was up to my mother to get me and my brothers packed and on the train for California. It was the first train I'd seen up close, and it was awe-inspiring. To me, it looked like some ancient monstrosity, spewing steam up into the sky. I held on tight to the hands of my mother and brother as we approached. I don't remember who lifted me up to get on the train, but I do remember the feeling of rising effortlessly into this strange, iron beast.

The train was also full of enlisted men, in transit from the war, but to which direction, I couldn't say. I do remember how they cat-called and wolf-whistled at my mother (a very beautiful and stylish woman in her day) even as she hustled two small children along in front of her while cradling an infant in her arms.

I remember walking down the train's narrow aisle and sliding into the seat. I had the window seat and I looked avidly out it as we began to move. Despite my excitement, I gave in to the gentle motions of the train, sleeping my way across the country. My next memory is of my mother waking us in Los Angeles's Union Station, where we were to meet up with our father.

When we first arrived in Los Angeles, we stayed with my father's sister, who owned a salon on First Street, not too far from L.A.'s Chinatown. She had a small apartment above the salon. We could see City Hall from the windows. That was where we all lived for a short time.

Coming as I did from Texas, it must have been the first time I'd really encountered large groups of Asian people, but I don't remember really registering that they were different or unusual. As a young boy, I didn't have a very good sense of the atmosphere in the country, or of the anti-Japanese sentiment, which was so pervasive then—especially on the West Coast. I didn't notice until my aunt pointed out to me how many of the locals wore small signs around their necks or buttons on their clothes proclaiming they were Chinese. I presume this was a way of forestalling any misaimed harassment. I certainly hope it worked for them.

During the week, both my parents would travel down to San Pedro (a distance of roughly thirty miles) where they would work in the plants, helping the war effort. They would stay there for the entire week, coming home on the weekends to visit us boys. In between weekends, our aunt would look after us while we did our best to keep busy.

Appropriately, it was in Los Angeles, home to Hollywood, where I discovered movies. At that time, Broadway (the main thoroughfare running through downtown Los Angeles) was rife with movie theaters, with perhaps three or four on every block. As my brother and I got bolder in our explorations of the city, the marquee lights inevitably drew us in.

I fell in love with cowboy pictures, doing my best to see every one of them. To make movie money, my brother and I would head out into the city with my shoeshine kits, charging ten or fifteen cents per pair of shoes. Some days, I would spend my nickel for the feature (plus another nickel for popcorn) and just sit inside the theater all day, watching the same movie over and over again until it was time to run back to my aunt's apartment for the evening.

It wasn't a perfect arrangement, what with our parents being gone so much of the time, but I didn't know at the time that our family was actually one of the luckier ones. The huge influx of new defense workers from all over the country had created an incredible need for housing, which the city of Los Angeles was scrambling to accommodate. New housing solutions were being developed, but not nearly fast enough. And in every new planned community, priority was always given to white defense workers. Many individuals, and sometimes entire families, had to make do with much less comfortable accommodations. Some were left to sleep on the streets.

We were lucky enough to eventually get a space at a new, planned community specifically for people who were working in the defense plants. Our neighbors would be my parents' coworkers.

It may have been a new development, but it was hardly palatial. Everything had been built quickly with an eye toward efficiency. The houses were more like shacks, not much larger than my aunt's apartment. In-home plumbing was literally a pipe dream. Instead, we shared a bathroom (including toilet, sink, and shower) with a number of other families. We also had a communal laundry room where everyone jostled to get their clothing washed.

It was around this time that our little family grew by one more with the birth of my new sister, Virginia Nell. We were now a family of six: my father, Nathaniel Durden Sr.; my mother, Connie; my older brother, Nathaniel Jr.; me; my younger brother, Sammy Joe; and the baby. As the youngest and only girl in the family, we all doted on little Virginia.

Amongst the other facilities that all the units all shared, there was an administration complex that also provided entertainment for the residents. On Saturdays, they would show a movie. Occasionally, I would be lucky enough that they would show a Western. Naturally, I really missed the Westerns that I'd eagerly watched back on Broadway.

The entertainment provided by the complex wasn't free. The Saturday movies cost five cents admission, which none of the local children could afford. But we didn't let that stop us. Instead, a group of kids from the neighborhood would get together and each of us would pitch in a penny to send a duly elected representative to the screening. When he came back, we'd all gather around him in a big circle while he acted out the whole plot for us, showing us exactly how the good guy had managed to find a new way to best the bad guy this time. I credit this experience and others like it with helping me to develop my imagination as a young man.

By this time, we had improved our situation somewhat—at least we were all together in the defense plant housing—but my parents were always on the lookout for something better. When the opportunity came along, we left the company housing and moved to Watts, to the then-new Jordan Downs housing project. The 700-unit apartment complex would eventually become famous, first as the birthplace of the infamous Crips gang, and second as one of the settings for the 1965 Watts Riots. But when we moved in, Jordan Downs was simply more housing for workers and one of the first projects designed for veterans returning from the war.

Of course, even then, there were still racial tensions in the air. Though the West didn't have the codified system of segregation that existed in many Southern states, there were very clear racial lines across the city that were enforced with economic, social, and political pressures. Jordan Downs was nominally open to families and individuals of any race, but it very rapidly became home to many people of color because they were barred from buying or renting in any other parts of town.

At the same time, the flood of Black Americans from the South to the West had continued. New arrivals to the city often wanted to settle in African American communities. Even if they didn't want to, L.A.'s powerful housing discrimination laws meant they didn't have many other options than to settle for what was available.

Unfortunately for the newest arrivals, the end of the war signaled the end of the well-paying defense jobs that had lured my father and thousands like him out to California. Just as with housing, Black men and women found that, even though there weren't

Jim Crow regulations in this state, there was still a great deal of employment discrimination. Though we had been part of the Great Migration, we found that social mobility in Los Angeles was nearly impossible.

The race situation in LA was a volatile mix, as the ensuing decades demonstrated. But for me, it was something different. I looked past a lot of the troubles, seeing the opportunities we were given and the situations that my family simply faced together. As a kid just starting to become really aware of the world around me, it was home.

That isn't to say it wasn't without peril. My mother was keenly aware of our family's safety at all times. She wanted to make sure that we were occupied and engaged so that we did not wander into dangerous situations. For that reason, she decided that each one of us was going to learn how to play an instrument. She let each of us boys (my sister was still a little too young for a musical career at this point) pick out an instrument that we wanted to play. She insisted that it was a good hobby that would encourage focus, patience, and discipline. Plus, we might even enjoy it. I chose the clarinet; my older brother took the trumpet; and my younger brother chose the trombone. We were pretty close to a jazz trio!

Twice a week, my brothers and I would take the streetcar (in those days, there was still reliable public transportation in L.A.) downtown for our lessons. The train line (called the Watts Local) went from Watts Station on 103rd Street all the way to the Pacific Electric Building downtown, stopping what felt like once every block.

When we first started taking lessons, my mother would ride the streetcar with us and wait while we practiced until it was time to be heading back home the same way. As we grew older and more familiar with the trip, she started allowing us to go on our own (not, of course, without getting a thorough polishing up at home before we were allowed to leave). She would call the music place before we left and tell them to expect us, and they, in turn, would call her when our lessons were finished so she could be waiting at the trolley stop when we returned.

She would walk us back home (about two miles), asking about our lessons and how we were progressing. She always made sure we were practicing like we were supposed to; she made us put hours into it, even when it felt like a chore. At first, the enforced practicing really annoyed me. But after a while, I actually started to look forward to it. I had moved past the novelty phase and I was starting to develop a genuine love for music.

It was around this time that my mother and father told us they were separating. It was a very hard time for everyone. They say that a divorce is like a death in the family, and that's exactly what it felt like for me. But even in the midst of it all, my mother insisted that we stick with our music.

Before all of this had happened, I'd asked my mother if I could make the switch from the clarinet to the saxophone. If I had known what was coming, I probably wouldn't have made the request; switching to the sax meant investing more money in another instrument. With Dad out of the house, our budget was tighter than ever, but hardship had never kept my mother from providing for her children. I don't exactly know how my mother made it happen, but she got me a beautiful e-flat alto saxophone. To this day, I still have it.

I was able to quickly acclimate to the sax, and I even learned to read music. With every lesson, I was getting better and better on both the saxophone and the clarinet. It got to the point that I was good enough to join the school band at Jordan High School (which housed grades seven through twelve at the time). I enjoyed playing in the band, most of all for the feeling of belonging. Between practice and performances, the kids in the band spent a lot of time together. In the morning, before school started, we would get together and just jam. We especially liked to play "Me and Mrs. Jones," a song that was popular at the time.

Our music teacher, Mr. Lippi, would leave the door open for us, and we often attracted a little crowd of curious onlookers. It became a little daily ritual, our mini-concerts before first period started. In many ways, my mother's plan to keep us busy and out of trouble had worked.

But the shelter of music wasn't enough. Soon, the lure of friendship and belonging grew incredibly strong, for both my brother and I, especially now that our father was more or less out of the picture. We both wanted to be with people who understood more than the joy of a few minutes of music in the morning.

The "El Camino Hawks" weren't a gang in the same way we think of street gangs today. They were more like a social club, and such groups (for both boys and girls) were popular in high schools all over the nation. There were, of course, other "clubs" that had more of a dark side and tended toward violent and criminal activities. But I never thought of the Hawks that way. We were a little rebellious, maybe, but we weren't bad kids.

One day, I was sitting in the bleachers with the rest of the Hawks while our gym teacher gave us instructions for the day's activities. I'm not sure exactly how the argument started, but before I knew it, one of my fellow Hawks was getting in an all-out brawl with another boy.

We didn't know it at the time, but our friend actually had been drinking already that day, and so the other fellow got the best of him pretty easily. Though the fight was quickly broken up, the other boy managed to give our friend a real beating.

Shortly after class, we decided to settle the score. A few of us found the other boy and jumped him in retaliation. It had seemed like the right course of action at the time; "an eye for an eye" just seemed to make sense. But it was the first real bit of serious violence I'd been involved in and, almost immediately, my conscience started to bother me.

I didn't like it; I didn't like any of it. I was fine when being a Hawk meant strutting around the school and feeling ten feet tall with my buddies, but I hadn't signed on for hurting other people. I figured that there had to be a better way to have friends and fit in. I just hadn't figured out what that was.

What I didn't realize was that "other way" had been right in front of me the whole time. As a member of the band, I spent a lot of time around the various sports teams at school. We played during the games and, sometimes, I would just sit in the bleachers and watch the football team practice. I always liked the strong sense of camaraderie that all the players seemed to have with one another.

I had never really thought of playing team sports before. At thirteen, I was still small, having not yet had my growth spurt. Just to look at me, no one would have said, "There's a football player." But I was drawn to the feeling of being part of a group—a group that, unlike the El Camino Hawks, was healthy rather than destructive.

When I approached the assistant coach and asked about going out for the team, he looked me up and down, and I knew what he was seeing: a scrawny boy with little to no formal athletic experience. Instead of turning me down, as I'm sure he wanted to, he told me to ask the head coach, which I promptly did.

"Sure," the head coach said. "Go see the coach of the B-team." The B-team was what we would call the freshman team today, filled with young, inexperienced, and undeveloped students. But I didn't see it as that. For me, it was an opportunity.

I went right out and got my physical in preparation for tryouts. I tried to approach this new endeavor the same way I had approached my music. I gave it my all and tried to improve my skills as much as possible.

After tryouts, I was given a uniform and I became part of a team. It was, unbeknownst to me at the time, a life-changing moment. Wearing that uniform was a very tangible way of joining a group and signifying to everyone that I was part of something bigger than myself. It would also set me down the path of a lifelong career in football.

My first game was against Westchester High School. Westchester was a fairly new high school (it had just opened in 1948) and this was the first year our football team had played them, so no one really knew what to expect. I was the starting defensive tackle and, even though I was new to the team, I had a really good game. I was very pleased with my performance, but I was even more pleased when, the following Monday, the school's newspaper came out with a small article about all of the sporting events of the previous weekend. There, in black and white, was my name and a short description of some of the things I'd done during the game. It was just a little note, but the paper praised my performance, and I was bowled over at the idea of appearing in the newspaper at all.

It was easy to drift away from the El Dorado Hawks. Once I had discovered that I could be good at sports, and that I could get friendship and acknowledgment and community from athletics, I knew I'd found what I was missing. I went out for just about any sport a student could go out for, even at one point trying out for the gymnastics team!

Between band, track, and football, I was busy almost all the time. Even if I'd had the time, I wouldn't have wanted to spend it with the Hawks. I no longer felt comfortable doing the things they wanted to do, and it seemed that I had suddenly changed a lot while they were just standing still, repeating the same patterns over and over again.

When I was in the ninth grade, my family moved again, this time to Boyle Heights. In the early 1950s, Boyle Heights had been a diverse neighborhood, traditionally home to Jewish, Japanese, and Hispanic residents. However, heavy redlining (when banks refuse to offer loans for property in certain geographic areas, usually minority neighborhoods) was driving out anyone who could afford to live elsewhere.

By the time my family moved to Boyle Heights, it was almost entirely Hispanic. As one of the few Black families in the area, we were conspicuously different. But that never entered into my mind. My main concern was that the move forced me to change schools. My sporting career at my new school, Roosevelt High, was a new beginning. I was in the ninth grade now, and I knew that expectations would be different for me.

When I was still at Jordan, I had befriended a guy named Ron Struthers, who was very talented with the shot put. I was curious about other track events, so I asked him to help me learn. He was a great teacher, showing me how to go across the ring and how to use my momentum properly. Under his tutelage, I became pretty darn good at the shot put, even challenging the city record at one point.

Because of my age, I had always used an eight-pound shot; but when I got to Roosevelt and they saw how I was performing, they immediately moved me to varsity shot put, where I was required to use a twelve-pound shot. Suddenly, my scores weren't quite as impressive. So that was my first real lesson in how things were going to change as I got older and more serious about sports.

For all that, I was settling in well at Roosevelt, running track and playing football, although there was a certain tension in the background. Boyle Heights was heavily gang-affiliated, and the gangs there were a lot more serious than the El Camino Hawks. I tried to stay away from that world as much as possible, but sometimes it was unavoidable.

One day, I was walking home from school through Elysian Park when I came across a group of boys who were roughly my age.

They were crowded together and I couldn't see exactly what they were doing. Frankly, I didn't want to. It wasn't my business; I was just trying to get home. None of them said anything to me or acknowledged my presence, but they stared me down until I had walked out of sight.

It might have been just another odd but harmless incident, except that my younger brother came walking along the same way just a few minutes later. My brother was younger and smaller than me, and he was a much easier target for the bigger boys. They attacked him and chased him all the way home, beating him with belts as they went. By the time he made it home, he was covered in welts from being struck with hard metal belt buckles.

The next day at school, some of the other kids were able to shed at least a little light on what had happened. According to them, I had not been attacked because my status as a good athlete had bought me a little bit of credit from gangs affiliated with the school. That protection, unfortunately, did not extend to my little brother.

It was the first serious incident of its kind but, for my mother, once was enough. We hadn't been living in Boyle Heights very long, but she decided that day that we would be moving out as soon as we could. I couldn't help but think of my own brush with "gang" life. Even though the Hawks weren't as serious as those boys in Elysian Park, I still felt an old twinge of guilt about my behavior back then and a considerable sense of relief that I was no longer involved with those kinds of activities.

We quickly relocated to 48th Street where, for the first time, we had our own home. It was a beautiful place. With three bedrooms and two baths, it was like heaven after years of shoebox apartments. Once again, my mother had worked a financial miracle, preparing a beautiful home for us even without the help of a second income.

Our new address put us smack in the middle between two different high school districts: Jefferson High School, which was a traditional secondary school—one of the oldest in the city, in fact—and Manual Arts High School, which had more of a technical or vocational focus. We were each allowed to pick which school we'd like to attend. My older brother chose Jefferson, as would my younger brother, when the time came. I was the odd man out, selecting Manual Arts, where I hoped to continue my flourishing sports career. Later, my little sister would follow in my footsteps and attend Manual Arts.

Earnel Durden – Manual Arts High School in 1955

While we were navigating our way through new schools, our mother was also making changes. She had done so much for us ever since the divorce, stretching a dollar to incredible lengths to make sure that we had a secure home and a good education, as well as the "extras" that we needed. So when she told us that she was getting ready to re-marry, we were glad for her. For a long time, she had been struggling alone, and we were happy to see that she had found someone.

From this marriage, my second sister was born. My mother named her Condicia Renee Dumas. Even though this meant Virginia was no longer the only girl in the family, she was elated to have a little sister; we were all so happy, and we loved her so much. I thought Condicia was a blessing to our family.

By the time I entered my new high school, my reputation had preceded me a bit. Coaches had heard about my performance at Jordan and Roosevelt, so I knew that they were expecting a lot from me. At the time, I was still trying to hang on to the school band, even with all of my other commitments. But as I got more serious with athletics, that situation became increasingly untenable. I knew I was going to have to make a choice, and I was reaching a point in my life when the things I chose to focus on could well become the things I spent my adult life pursuing.

Though I enjoyed it and I was even pretty good at it, I gave up music. I had reached a point where I could play virtually any reed instrument, but I knew that my passion for music wasn't the same as my passion for sports. While I had a knack for music, I thought my potential football talent was even greater.

There was a young man, another fellow band member, named H.B. Barnum, whom I had always admired. He was an incredible musician, even when we were still in high school. He could walk into the band room and play every instrument, a feat that always amazed me. He wasn't just talented, though; he was incredibly dedicated, and he was always working on his skills. Eventually, he grew up to be a well-known musician and played for many years on *The Tonight Show*.

When I looked at H.B. Barnum, I knew that I wasn't serious about music the way he was. But I felt that I could be that kind of serious about football. From that day on, I decided to put all of my focus on becoming a better and more effective player. I didn't know it then, but that decision in that moment would come to define most of my adult life.

CHAPTER TWO

Big Games and Big Decisions

igh school was one of the early highlights of my life. Over the course of those four years, I discovered my true passion. It was then that I began to realize I was engaged in what would be my life's work.

Going to Manual Arts every day often felt like stepping into a different world. At home, I had never thought seriously about sports or about my own athleticism. I didn't come from a family of athletes, although my mother had told us that my father was a great baseball player in his youth. Apparently, he would stand at the plate for two strikes before easily knocking the ball out of the park on what would have been the third strike. He actually attracted the interest of the manager of a local barnstormer team. These are sports teams that travel from place to place outside the structure of a particular "league." Because they were unaffiliated, a barnstorming team's game was, legally, more like a show than a sporting event. Many of the Negro League teams barnstormed in the early days.

The manager offered to pay my father to travel with his team, but I guess Dad just wasn't sufficiently interested in the sport. Similarly, my brothers probably could have played sports, but that was just never where their interests lay. We tended to do other things when we were together.

At Manual Arts, however, I was consumed with thoughts of how to get better, how to compete, and how to sharpen my skills. I imagine that most young people who grow up admiring the successful athletes around them think that they came up amongst the truly exceptional. I'm not immune to this way of thinking, either.

In my case, though, I was lucky enough to attend high school with some unequivocally gifted men and women who always kept me on my toes. Even though I spent twenty years in the NFL and coached at various other institutions, the people I looked up to in my boyhood still stand out in my mind. Ken Dennis was one of them. Ken and I went to different high schools, but we were always in competition with each other. During this time, he was running a 9.3- and 9.4-second hundred-yard dash. Even though he was still in high school, his times were some of the best in the nation amongst both high school and college runners.

There were also the McNeil brothers, Charles and Ettis, a pair of 168-pound guards who played both offense and defense. Charles eventually went on to the National Football League and, when I was working with the San Diego Chargers, I saw some of the records that Charles had set were still on the books—and still unbroken. Similarly, my friend Charles Dumas became the first man in the world to clear seven feet in the high jump (he used the "straddle technique," as it was called then), doing so when he was only in the eleventh grade.

On my high school football team, I was surrounded by amazing sportsmen like Bob Allan, Grant Gridiron, Bush Manson, and Willard Penn, just to name a few.

We had other talent, like Ted Bates, who graduated with me from Oregon State University (he later went on to play for the Chicago Cardinals, before they became the St. Louis Cardinals and

Me at the 50th Reunion of Manual Arts High (class of 1955). Starting from the left, Bush Manson, Earl Jones, Grant Gridiron, Bob Allan, and Earnel Durden. The woman is Willard Penn's wife—Willard unfortunately passed away about a month before, so his wife took his place.

finally the Phoenix Cardinals). One of my other friends, Paul Lowe, (who played at Oregon State University with Ted and I) went on to play with the 49ers and San Diego Chargers. He was one of the best athletes I've ever seen in my life. Even our competition was gifted. Lee Sampson, who went on to play professional football up in Canada, attended Centennial High School during that same period, and he was simply incredible. All around me was talent, both on my team and on the opposite side of the field.

Our track team was equally impressive. We won the state championship during my last year of high school. At state, we had preliminaries in the morning and finals in the afternoon. In the morning, our Manual Arts team managed to break the eight-man-mile relay interscholastic high school record. Then, in the afternoon, we broke our own record from the morning!

That record only stood one year, however. During my freshman year at Oregon State, some friends from back in Los Angeles sent word to me that Jefferson High School had broken our relay record. If we had to lose the record, though, I couldn't imagine a better team to lose it to. The relay team's leader was Willye White, who would later go on to represent the United States five times in the Olympics.

It wasn't just the young men who were setting records, though. A girl on the track and field team named Earlene Brown really caught my attention. She was probably the largest woman I'd ever seen in my life—6'1" and 240 pounds. She was incredibly powerful and, in her later career, she also represented the US in several Olympics as a shot putter. As you'd imagine, she was dedicated and tough. Even though she was active in sports at a time when it was less common for women to be competitive, no one—boy or girl—messed with Earlene. I first met Earlene in the seventh grade at Jordan High School and, even at that tender age, she could hold her own against anyone who came along.

These other students had a profound effect on me as I was coming into my own on the football field and on the track. Despite our loyalties to our own teams, we all worked to improve ourselves. That's the magic of organized sports. I had to constantly push myself because I saw how high the standards were, and that there were others striving to do more. I was performing next to dedicated, skilled athletes, and it was important for me to maintain my status in the school and with other groups.

That was a big reason I never dabbled in substance abuse. I always thought of myself as only just being able to compete with the stars of the various teams. I believed that any impairment of my skills, no matter how slight, might be just enough to take away what I was working toward, enabling the others to quickly leave me behind. This desire to always compete to the absolute best of my ability allowed me to steer away from destructive habits during some of the most vulnerable years of my life, and I've always been thankful for the good precedent that I set in those years.

I was able to keep pushing myself as hard as I could because, as time went on, I was seeing the benefits of my work on the field—and in the classroom. Our football team had a long string of successes, and I was so happy to be part of that. By the time my senior year rolled around, I wanted to give the team my absolute all and go out knowing I had tried my hardest. I also wanted to win.

When I was a junior, we played San Fernando High in the city championship—and they whooped us. I don't think I've ever been hurt so badly by a loss. The whole team felt it, and I knew that every man on that team was thinking the exact same things that I was thinking. What could we have done differently? How could we have turned that game around? Our only comfort was the knowledge that we would be facing them again next season—but unfortunately, the seniors would not have that chance. My under-classmen teammates and I would have a chance to redeem what had happened. We resolved that we would be ready for them in the next season.

My senior year, we opened the season with a practice game against North Hollywood. San Fernando was scheduled for the week as the season opener. I can tell you, most of us weren't really "in the moment" when we went up against North Hollywood. We'd all been obsessing over San Fernando for a year, and now that they were only a week away, we could hardly think about anything else. That especially included North Hollywood who, in our opin-ion, hadn't done much to distinguish themselves in recent games.

Our lack of focus hurt us in the game, and North Hollywood was able to beat us. Even that, though, seemed less vivid and import-ant than the upcoming San Fernando game. Of North Hollywood, we generally just figured we'd meet them in the playoffs and have our second chance there to bring them back to Earth (as it turned out, North Hollywood didn't make the playoffs that year, so we never did actually get the chance to face them again).

The week following our loss to North Hollywood, we played San Fernando on our home field at Manual Arts. The spectator turnout was huge. By now, our rivalry was big news, and the game had been written up in all the papers. In addition to all the people from Manual Arts, San Fernando also had a big fan contingent coming in from the Valley. The place was packed and expectations were sky high.

It was a terrific game—we wound up beating San Fernando 25 to 13. After that game, it was like someone had lit a rocket under my team. We plowed through other schools: Venice, Fremont, Garfield, Washington, and Jefferson. We were unstoppable.

DANCING DURDEN BREAKS LOOSE TO SET UP TOILER TOUCHDOWN

Fullback Earnel Durden sweeps right end for 24 yards in second quarter to set up Manual's first touchdown in stunning 25-13 upset over San Fernando, defending city champ, yesterday at Manual. Conrad Johnson and Lanny Lafferty made futile grabs at Toiler ace.

Newspaper clipping featuring that game

It was during the Jefferson game that our coach, Jim Blewett, taught me something that I've employed well into my own coaching career. Coach Blewett was definitively "Old School," a real Knute Rockne kind of guy. He'd give us those growling pep talks about how, "We're gonna run inside of 'em! We're gonna run outside of 'em!" It might have been a bit cheesy, but it did always get us fired up.

What I'll never forget, though, were his astute strategies, which I'd never encountered before. For example, in that game, he told us to go up to the line of scrimmage.

"I want you all to line up in a two-point stance," he said. "Put your hands on your knees and make sure you can see everything. I want you to look and see how every defensive man is lined up, whether he's on your nose, whether he's in a gap. You get all that information and then call time out."

I thought this idea was fantastic—we'd be able to fully assess the team's defensive strategy based on their positioning and then we could modify our own play based on what we saw. And that's exactly what we did.

Before the game, we had heard they were running an Eagle 4-4 defense on us. We were skeptical, though, because that wasn't what they had been doing all year. So we did as Coach Blewett had instructed and carefully examined the defensive positions.

"Sure enough, Coach," we said, "they are running an Eagle 4-4."

They had planned on changing it up on us and were hoping to take advantage of the element of surprise. Instead, Coach Blewett sent Bush Manson up the middle for about ten yards. He came back and I went around the end to score the touchdown.

I scored three touchdowns by halftime, giving us a lead of 21 to 0. By that time, the crowd had also started to turn against us, or against me in particular. They started throwing things down at us. At first, it was mostly harmless trash, but then glass bottles and cans starting raining down from the stands. I could hear the chanting in the crowd: "KILL NUMBER 40!" That was my number. The strong negative reaction started to worry Coach Blewett, so he actually had me sit out the second half, just to be safe. I sat there covered with the team's poncho and just watched the rest of the game.

Even still, we still beat them 32 to 0.

When we played Roosevelt High, where I had briefly attended school, we had a funny moment in the parking lot after the game. Our team was out near the bus. As we milled around, taking off our cleats and getting ready to head out, I noticed a heavyset man running flat out toward us from across the lot. He was moving so fast that my first thought was, "Oh man, what have we done now?"

As he got closer, however, I recognized him as my former principal, Mr. Dougherty. Far from being angry, he actually wanted to pay us a compliment. "I just wanted to congratulate you guys," he said. "This is the best high school football team I've ever seen." It felt a little bit like I had come full circle, getting that kind of affirmation from an official at my former high school. We won the game 52 to 13.

We went through our league undefeated, which was no easy task. The Southern League was considered the toughest league in the city at that time. After that, we were on our way to the playoffs, playing Lincoln and Bell High Schools. Both schools presented challenges for our team, but we won both games. With those victories, we began gearing up for the championship.

The championship game was the last, most significant game of my last, most significant year in high school, and I was feeling the pressure. The night before, I didn't get a wink of sleep. Coach Blewett had instructed us to be at the school by 9 a.m., even though the game was scheduled for 1 p.m. I found myself walking to the school at 7 a.m. because I couldn't take lying awake in bed anymore.

I was feeling this kind of uneasy tension creeping across my entire body, but as I drew closer to the school, I saw other players filtering in. I wasn't the only one who had been too anxious to sleep.

We were playing Los Angeles High School, a team from the Western League. They were a good team with a great coach by the name of Harry Edleson. They had gone through their league undefeated, just as we had. The game was being held at the Los Angeles Coliseum, which made it feel even more prestigious. Despite the jitters, we played a strong game and eventually shut out Los Angeles High 32 to 0. We scored two touchdowns, which were called back. I scored two of the touchdowns of those twenty-one points!

Despite the importance of sports in my high school life, athletics weren't everything. There was at least one other important discovery I made in those days that would impact me for the rest of my life. During my time between classes, my teammates and I would sit in the quad and just "people watch." Admittedly, we may have watched the girls a bit more than the guys. On one of these days, I saw a young lady walk by, I couldn't say exactly why, but I was just drawn to her. I knew I had to talk to her. So I went right up to her and introduced myself. I found out that her name was June Earlene Pecot. She was the woman who would one day become my wife.

June Durden

I had dated other girls before, but I'd never been in a truly serious relationship. I had liked those girls, but I hadn't felt anything like I did with June. The more I learned about June, the more I liked her.

Like me, she was a transplant to the city. She had actually been born in New Orleans, one of six children. Her father was a porter for the famed Pullman Cars, and the family had moved often to accommodate his work. Her oldest sister, Marion, had been sixteen, while Justin and Joseph, her two older brothers, were also young teens when their parents divorced. Her brothers and Marion left the house a few years later to pursue adult life. June had been only eight, so she and her two younger siblings, Sammy and Teddy, stayed with their mother. The divorce was challenging for June's mother, who had a difficult time coping and trying to keep up with three young children.

Eventually, the stress became too much for June's mother, and she suffered a nervous breakdown. June and her two younger siblings were sent to stay with other family members until their mother could recover. By this time, June's oldest sister, Marion, had finished nursing school and had found a job in one of LA's largest hospitals, so June was able to live with her.

Luckily for me, Marion had made the decision to enroll June in Manual Arts High School.

Some time passed before June's family was whole again. As June and I grew closer, I started meeting her family, and they really embraced me—especially her mother. I'm not sure exactly why, but June's mother and I clicked right away. She had met and rejected some of June's suitors before, but we sort of just fell in love right away. I would go over to their house to play cards, and June's mom and I would always be partners against June and her brother. I called her Mama Pecot and, to the day she died, she was one of my very favorite people.

I liked June tremendously, but we were still very young. We kept our relationship pretty casual throughout high school, and we were free to date others, if we wished. We didn't get really serious until my junior year of college. After I graduated from Oregon State, we got married. Now, after more than fifty years and three children, I'm still just as taken with her as I was that day in the quad.

My happiness now is founded in the awareness that, as I neared the end of my high school career, I was making decisions that were going to impact the rest of my life. Suddenly, I had to weigh everything very carefully, and I increasingly found that I was without a guide. My parents could only do so much when it came to making choices about higher education. When they were young people, it just wasn't feasible for working-class African Americans to go to college. I had their unwavering support, as they wanted the best for me, but they couldn't offer me any advice on what I might face. Any choice I made would be a little bit of a gamble. Those choices were mine alone.

I also knew that my career choices would be constrained, at least to some degree, by the racist structures in America that prevented Black men and women from holding certain jobs. When I was younger, I had been very interested in the idea of being an FBI agent. I would have been a good candidate—I was smart, honest, and physically fit. I was told, however, that FBI jobs simply weren't an option for men of color. It was one of many paths closed to me just because of the color of my skin.

When I first conceived the idea of writing a book, I thought a lot about how my story could be valuable to people, especially young people. I wanted to share my personal experiences across decades in the world of college and professional football. More than that, I wanted to give people a real sense of what the world was like when I was growing into adulthood.

Young people of color today are often incredibly focused on our current racial issues here in America, which are significant and important. However, I think that we sometimes fail to really educate our youth about what a harrowing journey it has been to get African Americans to where they are today. Obviously, I'm not implying that our work is done. But we have made incredible strides, and we sometimes forget about that. We focus on progress, and we often forget to highlight the individual sacrifices of so many that made that progress a reality.

I remember that summer day when several of my friends took the buses to Selma, Alabama and the streets of Mississippi to march in protest. I remember, too, how they suffered for their integrity. They were beaten with batons, bitten by dogs, and faced awful abuses one could only imagine. But for them, it wasn't imaginary. My friends were somewhat "lucky" in that they came back alive and weren't imprisoned, but many of them were never the same again. Even if their physical wounds healed, they carried other, deeper scars for the rest of their lives.

Today, we often think of activism during the Civil Rights period as heroic—which it was—and something that people should be proud of—which they should be. But we must remember that it was also incredibly traumatic. It cost them something, those brave men and women who took a stand against hatred. We must teach our children to understand and honor that sacrifice.

When I was completing my high school career and starting to think about the future, I was doing so against the backdrop of ongoing desegregation in education. The Supreme Court decision on *Brown v. Board of Education* was in 1954, just a year before I graduated from high school. Many colleges were still Whites-only in practice, if not in law. In 1957, my sophomore year of college, Governor Orval Faubus famously ordered the Arkansas National Guard to prevent a group of African-American students from entering Little Rock Central High School.

Manual Arts had a White majority at the time that I was there. It had been a bit strange for me in the beginning, because I had always gone to very diverse schools with large minority populations. At Manual Arts, I was one of relatively few non-White students. There was me, a handful of other Black students, some Asians, and a few Hispanic kids. Despite this, I had never felt particularly unwelcome because of my race, even though I was always acutely aware of how few boys and girls of color were around me.

I remember being completely fascinated when Centennial High School in Compton hired its first Black coach, Aaron Wade. He wasn't just Centennial's first Black coach—he was actually the first Black coach in the county of Los Angeles. The Centennial team always attracted attention because Coach Wade had instituted a behavior code, along with cultivating a great football team. His athletes had a dress code for game days: red sweaters, white shirts, and black pants. You could always identify a member of the Centennial football team, whether it was on campus or in the community, and Coach Wade's students took a great deal of pride in this tradition.

Later, Aaron Wade would go on to become one of the first African-American officials in the NFL. For young men of color who wanted a career in sports, Wade was a legend. We didn't have a lot of people like him—Black men in positions of authority in the sports that we loved—to look to as an example.

My life revolved around sports, family, classes, and my friends; if there were White kids at Manual Arts that had a problem with Black students, they didn't make themselves known for me. The football team was mostly White as well, but we were all unified by a desire to go harder and do better on the field. I even hung out a few times with some of the guys on the team, which was also different for me. Before that, I'd never really had White friends, just acquaintances. We bonded over our shared love of the game and our collective goals for the team's future.

Growing up in mostly Black neighborhoods, I'd spent much of my life somewhat insulated from the kind of direct, overt racism that the Civil Rights movement was combating. It wasn't until just after graduating from high school that I got my first taste of true racism.

In the summer of 1955, I had been invited to play in two all-star games. The first game was the "Shrine" game, held at the Los Angeles Coliseum. I always consider this game a fun one in my life, because I got the chance to play with a lot of guys who I had usually played against in high school. It was fun to band together rather than be enemies.

The game was huge—it was the southern California selected all-star athletes pitted against the all-stars selected from northern California. That particular year, there was a player by the name of Dick Bass, and he was *the* all-star of northern California. The papers labeled him in the same class as a superstar, and he was the biggest name player that we were starting against. I was happy to see my high school coach, Jim Blewett as one of the main coaches training our team; Aaron Wade was the other coach. I wanted to learn as much as possible from the both of them during this game.

In the summer of 1955, I joined the Southern California All Stars Football team, Southern California Shrine Team vs. Northern California. The two coaches were Jim Blewitt (left side) and Aaron Wade (right side). I am number 33 above!

We played on July 29, 1955, and we won the game!! It was quite a lifetime experience. Charles McNeil, number 25 in the previous picture—the 168-pound guard I mentioned earlier—was the player of the game. Dick Bass went on to play for the Rams, and was All-Pro for many years after that.

I had also been invited to play in the Breitbard game, a matchup between the Los Angeles City All-Stars and the CIF (California Interscholastic Federation) All-Stars. Both Ted Bates—one of the few other Black players on the Manual Arts team—and I were asked to participate. The game was to take place in San Diego. My team was the guest of the United States Marine's Recruiting Depot, while the United States Naval Depot hosted the CIF All-Stars. As a kid with no real familiarity with the military, it was fascinating to watch the Marines march everywhere they went—even to lunch and dinner!

The game was played in the massive Balboa Stadium, which had also housed all sorts of sporting events, not to mention baseball legends like Babe Ruth and Ty Cobb. For the occasion, everyone on the team was given beautiful blue jackets with white sleeves that were trimmed in red. Everything about this game felt special. It was more ceremonial than any of the other games I'd played in high school.

After the game was over, the team stopped at a local restaurant so we could eat before we headed home. In those days, the route between San Diego and Los Angeles was just a two-lane highway. The journey between the two cities took hours.

Nothing about the restaurant seemed unusual. It didn't have any of those "WHITES ONLY" signs that have since become such a powerful symbol of the segregation era. Nevertheless, there was something quietly hostile in the air as soon we sat down.

Ted and I were the only people of color in the group. When we took a table along with the rest of the players, it was clear that we were definitely part of the team—after all, we had those matching jackets. No one said anything to us. Ted and I watched as the wait-resses carefully took everyone else's order but ours. When we tried to speak up, the waitresses either looked right through us or simply turned and walked away.

Drinks were brought out. Then entrees. It became increasingly clear to Ted and I that they weren't going to take our orders. They were refusing us service and pretending that we didn't exist. While the wait staff ignored us, the rest of the patrons were watching our every move, wondering if we'd react or take the hint. We were acutely aware that everyone was watching us.

It's hard to express the profound sense of shame I felt in that moment, as though I'd broken some rule I didn't even realize existed. That was one of the most frustrating and painful things about discrimination. Somehow, it makes you feel as though you've done something wrong, even when you're the one being explicitly mistreated.

Ted and I didn't know what to do, so eventually we just left and waited outside while our teammates finished their meals. I had heard about this sort of thing happening in the South, but this was California. It was a new experience for me. I had never encoun-tered a situation like this before, and it came as a terrible shock, like a punch to the stomach. I can't tell you the name of the restaurant or exactly where in the city it was located, but to this day, I can still conjure up that queasy feeling of being ashamed.

Ted wasn't any more equipped to handle that sort of overt rac-ism than I was. It was awkward and humiliating, and neither of us knew what to say, so we just stood there in the Southern California sunshine, silent together.

As awful as that evening was, my high school experience could have been so much worse. In other states, I might have been barred from attending a school with any White students. I might have been restricted to schools with less funding and worse facilities. I might have been unable to compete with athletes of other races. I could have watched as innumerable doors were shut against me.

The fact that I had the option not only to go to college, but also to select from the ones that were courting me, was significant. Across the nation, people were already fighting and dying, enduring terrible pain to secure the access that I was being given. This was only due to my geographical location and my talent as an athlete. I was not unaware of what was going on in other parts of the country, and I kept that knowledge in the back of my head as I tried to decide where I wanted to attend college.

The recruiting grew intense as I neared the end of high school. I was inundated with piles of mail from college recruiters and coaches trying to woo me to join their teams. I fielded offers from all over the country. For the most part, though, I hadn't thought too seriously about leaving California.

I did briefly flirt with the idea of going to Lincoln University, a historically Black university in Missouri, where two of my teammates were headed. I liked the idea of going to an all African-American school. I thought it would be fun. But in the end, my thoughts always came back to the one school that had loomed large throughout my adolescence: UCLA.

UCLA had been a powerhouse when I was growing up. Coach Red Sanders led the team to a national championship in 1954 (to this date, it is still UCLA's only national championship). Under his watch, the team was churning out athletes like Primo Villanueva (the famous "Calexico Kid"), Sam "First Down" Brown, and 1953 All-American Paul Cameron. These were my heroes when I was a boy.

Plus, there was a pageantry to the school's program that I loved. New Year's Day in Los Angeles was all about college football. People would stream into the streets of Pasadena to watch the Rose Parade and support their team. I wanted to be a part of that big, communal celebration.

There was also one more major consideration: the Rose Bowl. For me, the Rose Bowl was the highlight of my college football. For years, I had dreamed of playing in it, and it was high on my list of goals for my college career. Thus, any school that didn't compete in the Rose Bowl could be easily dismissed.

It seemed as though everything were falling into place. I was most interested in UCLA, and UCLA (in the person of backfield coach Tommy Prothro) was also interested in me. It was all smooth sailing until, suddenly, Coach Prothro left his position at UCLA in favor of a head coaching job at Oregon State University.

For weeks, Coach Prothro had been recruiting me, mostly via his associate, Horace Johnson. All this time, he had been pushing me towards UCLA. Horace Johnson, who was also Black, was particularly adept at embedding himself in the lives of the players that he was courting. Our family had come to trust him over the course of the recruitment process.

When he visited to break the news to me, I could tell before he even started speaking that this was serious. "I know that going to UCLA has always been a dream of yours. I know that you have your heart set on going there," he said.

"Yes," I answered slowly, a little worried about where the conversation was heading.

"Well, I wanted to let you know that Coach Prothro is taking a head coaching job at Oregon State. And, as part of his recruiting team, I'm going with him."

I was silent after he said this. I wasn't sure what, if anything, this meant for me. Was I not being recruited for UCLA anymore?

But Horace continued: "He wants to take you to Oregon State with him. With us. Is that possible?"

I told him, quite frankly, that I didn't know. In all my thinking about college plans, I had never once considered Oregon State. I didn't know anything about the school or the team. The only thing I knew was that Coach Prothro was there and, apparently, he wanted me to be there as well.

Horace gave me time to think, but he didn't disappear. He spent a lot of time with my mom, trying to convince her that Oregon State was the best choice for me. He argued that it would be good for me to get out of Los Angeles and meet new people, see new things. I'd been a city boy for most of my life, and small-town living might broaden my horizons.

My mother liked Horace, and she saw merit in his arguments. But she knew that, in the end, the decision was mine to make.

I went to her once and asked for advice. "I don't know what to do," I said. "I like Coach Prothro a lot, but I just don't know about Oregon."

"I wish I knew what to tell you," she said, "but I don't. The only thing that I can do is pray for you and hope that you make the right decision."

I realized then that I was moving beyond my parents' realm of experience and, going forward, I would have to cut my own path. I started asking my teammates, trying to get a feel for where everyone was planning to attend college. Lincoln, University of Denver, Colorado State ... no one was headed to Oregon.

Then Ted Bates approached me. He had also been offered a scholarship to Oregon State and he was seriously considering it. This buoyed me a little; I liked the idea of having at least one familiar face in Oregon. I decided to take the leap. I decided to follow Tommy Prothro to Oregon State.

At that time, there was a strange phenomenon that sometimes occurred between an athlete's recruitment and his enrollment at a new school: he might get poached. Desirable players would be intercepted—either accidentally or deliberately—by representatives from other colleges, and wooed away before they ever even set foot on their intended campus.

On the Oregon State football team, we had a player named Sam Wesley who had been heavily recruited by the University of Oregon. It had been a done deal; he'd even gotten on the bus to U of Oregon. Unfortunately, he got off at the wrong stop and wound up at Oregon State. Seeing that a golden opportunity had been dropped into their lap, the Oregon State football team snapped him up on the spot. He never did make it to the University of Oregon.

There were three players that Coach Prothro had recruited from my area: me, Ted, and a guy named Paul Lowe. Tommy and Horace were determined to get us to our new homes with no unfortunate detours, so instead of taking a bus or a train where other recruiters might have been lurking, we all drove up to Oregon in Horace Johnson's brand new Mercury.

Needless to say, with three burly football players plus Horace, his wife, and their young son in the car, it was a little bit cramped. But we all made it to Corvallis, Oregon together, without incident.

We arrived on campus near dusk, having enough time to take a walk around and familiarize ourselves, grateful for the opportunity to stretch our legs. We were tired after our long drive, so we saved the more time-consuming exploration for another day.

At the time, I knew very little about the state of Oregon. I could see just from our brief walk that our campus (and the surrounding town) was overwhelmingly, almost exclusively, White. As it turned out, that was by design.

From its earliest inception, Oregon had some of the most explicitly anti-Black laws on the books outside of the Jim Crow South. This was a fact I had not known before agreeing to attend Oregon State. While many Northern states had successfully excluded African Americans and other people of color from living there by enforcing strict social ostracism, Oregon took it a step further and actually wrote it into their state constitution. Until 1926, Black Americans were legally prohibited from settling in Oregon, and that ban was rigidly enforced.

Even in major cities like Portland, White residents thought of the state as a fundamentally "White" place. They employed the usual discriminatory housing and banking practices to confine the few African-American residents to tiny areas, habitually bulldozing those same settlements whenever it was time to build or expand the city. They levied illegal fines and fees against the tiny handful of Black-owned businesses that cropped up in an effort to otherwise push any non-White persons out of the state.

They were enormously successful. At one point, the Oregon branch of the Ku Klux Klan disappeared, simply because there weren't enough minorities left in the state to intimidate or threaten. During the War years, African Americans from the South had just as much reason, theoretically, to settle in Oregon as they did to settle in California—after all, there were plenty of defense jobs on the Oregon coast. But instead of Black neighborhoods and enclaves, African Americans in Oregon just found a sea of bewildered—and frequently hostile—White folks.

Even today, in 2015, Oregon is still very homogenous (African Americans are a dwindling 2 percent of the population). When I arrived there in 1955, Ted and I were two of the perhaps seven or eight Black students on campus. To say that we stood out would be putting it very mildly.

For all its ugly history, I didn't feel harassed or hated in Corvallis. Mostly, what I experienced was the simple ignorance that comes from just not knowing much about the world or all the different people in it.

The day after we arrived, Ted and I went for a walk in the downtown area. As we were strolling down the street, we passed a mother with her young son, who was probably no older than four or five. We had already attracted a certain amount of attention on our walk, but this little boy was staring at us like we had two heads apiece.

"Mommy!" he said loudly, tugging on his mother's hand. "Look at those big black men!" In his true child's fashion, he said this at top volume. His mother immediately looked at us, embarrassed and, I believe, a little afraid of how we might react.

Of course, we weren't angry at the boy's outburst. He was a child, and he had clearly never seen anyone with a skin tone darker than "light beige" before. In the 1950s, it was even pretty rare to see Black people in films and television, so we very well could have been the first men of color he had ever seen in his life.

For Ted and I, coming from one of the most diverse cities in the country, it was very strange to encounter people who had so little experience with anyone outside their own ethnic group. Our interaction with the little boy wasn't hurtful or shameful in the way that the San Diego restaurant experience had been. But, it was enough to give us the bizarre feeling of being aliens in a strange place, looked upon with a mixture of curiosity and trepidation.

I thought—not for the last time—about Lincoln University and my friends on the team who were headed there. There, they would be able to blend in and wouldn't be seen as anything other than normal students. They would not have to deal with extra scrutiny and all-consuming—though not malicious—curiosity. They probably felt right at home there, among people who understood their background and experience. I couldn't imagine that I'd ever be able to think of Oregon as my home.

I felt the smallest twinge of worry. Had one of the biggest decisions of my life turned into one of my biggest mistakes?

CHAPTER THREE

The Collegiate Life in Corvallis

don't know if I was ever more aware of my race than in that first year at Oregon State. Everywhere I went, I stood out. The people around me always seemed to notice my presence. Mostly, this manifested in some minor staring or in people giving myself and other Black players a wide berth on the streets. But some who were less restrained made their curiosity very plain.

Chuck Marshall, a teammate who later went on to play for the NY Giants, experienced this firsthand during a routine trip to the doctor. Because Corvallis was such a small town, the team doctor was also the town doctor. Chuck found himself in a waiting room full of folks not necessarily affiliated with the team or the school, including a woman and her small son.

Chuck didn't take much notice of the pair; instead, he stretched out with a magazine over his face, waiting for his name to be called. Then he started to feel a small but insistent tugging on the edge of the magazine. Out of the corner of his eyes, he could see the little boy standing silently beside him and pulling the edge of the magazine down to expose Chuck's face.

Figuring that either the mother would come to collect her son or the kid would get bored, Chuck just pulled the magazine back up over his face. The boy responded by tugging it down even harder, scrutinizing Chuck thoughtfully.

"Mommy!" the boy shouted suddenly, "Why do you make me wash my face when this man doesn't have to?"

Confronted with someone who looked so unlike anyone he had ever known, the boy had made the assumption that Chuck must simply have a lot of dirt on his skin. Chuck got a good laugh out of that one, but these incidents were never completely amusing. At the end of the day, White people in Corvallis seemed very comfortable invading our space to satisfy their own curiosity.

Even in our own living quarters, it sometimes felt as though we were under a microscope. Ted Bates and I bunked together for a while, and we used to keep our door open—as most students did—when we were in the room, studying or hanging out. Soon, we began to notice another student who would just linger in the doorway. He never asked us anything or came inside, and if we asked him what he wanted, he always just shrugged off the question. Eventually, we realized that he was simply watching us to try to find out what we were like.

He admitted that he had never seen Black people before, except in films, and we were nothing like Stepin Fetchit or similar minstrel characters. We didn't fit into any template he had for Blackness, and that made him very curious about us. He was especially bemused by the small picture of my girlfriend (who would later become my wife), which I kept on my desk. June is very light-skinned and, at first, our curious visitor couldn't believe that she was actually African American.

Over time, these repeated visits started to really get under Ted's skin. It's bad enough to feel gawked at when you're out on the street; it's another thing entirely to experience it in what is supposed to be your home. The next time the young man showed up at our door, Ted confronted him.

At 6 feet, 3 inches tall, Ted could certainly be intimidating when he wanted to be. "Listen here, white boy," he said, getting right in the other boy's face. "Do not come to our door again."

The boy's eyes went wide and he stammered out an apology, insisting that he hadn't meant any harm. That was true; he wasn't trying to shame or threaten us. He was just curious. Like those children we encountered, he simply didn't realize how uncomfortable his actions had made us.

Seeing his genuine contrition relaxed Ted a lot and, over time, the three of us actually became very good friends. We still talk often, even now, and we occasionally reminisce about those days and our unusual meeting.

That young man was an outlier, however. For the most part, the White student body didn't want anything to do with Black students. That was okay with me at the time—it was better to be ignored than attacked, at least. Still, I couldn't help but think longingly of what my life would have been like at a more diverse school.

I was able to make a few friends with White students who seemed friendly and didn't mind striking up a conversation. I found that young women were generally more willing to engage than boys (except for the boys on the football team). Our social circles were growing, but it seemed like a painfully slow growth. I frequently felt as though I found rejection everywhere I looked.

I was so demoralized, in fact, that I had actually decided to leave the school. I wanted to go back to a place where I could be just another face in the crowd instead of the obvious odd-man-out. I had even packed up my clothes. I was all ready to go when Coach Prothro came to talk to me.

If one were to make a list of unlikely mentors for a young Black man, Tommy Prothro would have to be near the top. He wasn't just a White Southerner, but a White Southerner of a particularly aristocratic class (his father, Doc Prothro, owned a minor league team out of his home state of Tennessee). Traditionally, the Prothro family wasn't the sort to have much to do with working class White people, let alone people of color. On paper, we should have had no way to connect with one another.

And yet, Tommy Prothro would go on to become almost a second father for me.

Before he came to talk to me that day, I was ready to buy my ticket out of Oregon. Coach Prothro didn't beat around the bush—he was always a man of few words—and he didn't pretend that race wasn't an issue. He spoke frankly about the challenges I would face because of my race, but he strongly encouraged me to stick it out, because he felt I could be really successful at Oregon State.

By the end of our talk, I knew one thing for sure: Even if every White person in the state of Oregon wanted me gone, there was at least one important person who would always have my back. It was my coach.

Around the same time, I had a similar, frank discussion with another important authority figure. This time, it was my chemistry professor. I was struggling in my chemistry course, partially because science wasn't really my area of interest and partially because I was still on the fence about my commitment to Oregon State. My issues with the class naturally showed up in my grades, and the professor asked me to meet him, one-on-one.

I don't know exactly what I was expecting—probably another warning wrapped in a pep talk of the sort that teachers have been giving flagging students since time immemorial. Instead, he said bluntly, "Earnel, you must pass this course."

My ears pricked up then. It sounded a little more dire than the usual, grade-based warning.

"If you fail this class," he continued, "your entire race will be blamed. People will say, 'Those people just don't have what it takes to succeed in a college atmosphere.' If it were a White student, it would be about the individual and their aptitude, but you don't have that luxury."

This idea was not new to me—I saw it in action regularly. I had never expected to hear it stated so plainly by a White professor, however. The boldness of his statement shocked me, but I couldn't deny that he was right. It wasn't fair, but it was true. When I became one of the first Black people to enter these very White places, I became a pioneer, but I also became a symbol for the White people around me, who would take my every move and apply it broadly to all African Americans.

The pressure was intense, but it was also energizing. I left that meeting determined to pass the class, and I have never forgotten that professor's words. I don't remember his name or what he looked like (or all that much about chemistry, to be honest), but I still think back on what he told me whenever I am confronted with a difficult situation in my life. The burden is heavy and frustrating, but it is better to acknowledge it than to ignore it. In case you're wondering, I went on to pass that chemistry class with flying colors!

After these two incidents, I threw myself wholeheartedly into student life at Oregon State. I took an ROTC (Reserve Officers Training Core) class, as was required of all incoming male students. There were three branches of service offered: Army, Navy, and Air Force. I chose the Air Force because it seemed like it was probably the easiest option. I spent many an afternoon marching around the campus in my uniform in the snow. I had fun with the class, but I already knew that I was not going to stay in the ROTC program through junior and senior years, as some other students did. If I had done that, I could have entered the armed services as a commissioned officer. But that was not the path for me. I wanted to continue to pursue football and see where it would take me.

Earnel Durden, 1956, in the OSU ROTC Air Force Program

I spent my first year in the dorms, but after that, I branched out to group housing on campus. I knew for a fact that I never would have been accepted in any of the White fraternities and, of course, there were no Black frats on campus at that time. Instead, I lived in a place called Heckart Lodge with sixty other house members and a house mother. The three years I spent there taught me many valuable lessons, from table etiquette to how to get along with others in close quarters.

The gentlemen in Heckart Lodge.
I am in the first row, fourth from the right.

During our meals, strict etiquette was required. There was a senior at every table who acted as a kind of enforcer, and we received
materials instructing us on what we should and should not do at
meal times. If we did anything rude or otherwise out of line, we
would be fined. For me (and for most of the other guys, I imagine),
it wasn't the money so much as the embarrassment of having to be
corrected that kept us on our toes. We also competed with students
at the other campus houses for the highest overall grade point average. Even within the houses, our individual grades were posted on
a bulletin board for everyone to see, ranked from highest to lowest.
I was determined that my name would never appear at the bottom
of that list.

I spent much of my early time at Oregon State getting my
equilibrium, adapting to the new place and, yes, to the new people.
There was one place, however, that always felt familiar: the football
field.

The coaches were pushing us hard, holding two practices per day. One was for the Varsity team to prepare for their upcoming game of the week, and the other was for the freshman team, who were not allowed to play with the upper classmen. Because of that prohibition, we had to schedule our three games of the year against the University of Oregon twice and University of Washington once. Those games were great practice. We won all three, and I learned a lot about my teammates in the process. The city of Corvallis was abuzz about us. The word was, Coach Prothro had recruited the best freshmen players in the history of the school. Everyone was eager to see what we could do.

Freshman year had been exciting, bewildering, challenging, and a thousand other things besides. By the time summer rolled around, I was ready to return to Los Angeles and spend some time with my family.

My father knew that I was looking for summer work, and he put me in touch with a friend who secured a job for me on his construction crew. I spent that summer building what is now known as Interstate 5. It may have sounded like a tough job, but that was actually what I wanted. The worst thing I could imagine was spending three months lying around at home and getting out of shape.

With all the heavy manual labor, I would remain conditioned even through the long break. We were working on the stretch of I-5 coming out of San Juan Capistrano. At the time, that area was nothing but orange groves as far as the eye could see. When the wind was just right, you could smell the ripe fruit.

The job also offered me one other big perk: I was able to afford a Chevy Bel Air, which became my pride and joy.

That fall, I reported back to Oregon State University ready to work hard and achieve even more during my sophomore year. Football season started in earnest as soon as I arrived. It was always the hardest time of the year, at least physically. We were doing two solid weeks of double-days (two practices per day)—and after a few days of those, all you wanted to do was sleep. However, because football season started several weeks before formal classes, my teammates and I were the only students occupying a deserted campus. So even if we'd had the energy for socializing, there was hardly anyone around to socialize with! After two weeks, though, the practices tapered off into single practice days, and that was always exciting because it meant that we were inching closer to the first game day.

We opened our exhibition season that year against the University of Missouri. We were headed to Missouri for the game on what would be my first airplane trip. Somehow, that idea didn't actually occur to me until we were already in the air. Boy, was I nervous!

Before the flight, I had been preoccupied worrying about the game itself and also about traveling to Missouri, which was a Southern state. I was wondering what sort of treatment we might encounter there. By this time, there were four other Black players making the trip with me. We had all heard horror stories about how other African-American players had been treated on trips to Southern states, but I trusted Coach Prothro. I just couldn't believe that he would put us in any situation where we would be threatened or humiliated.

I was right, as it turned out. We played the game without incident and promptly headed back home. I found the plane ride much less stressful the second time. Our second game was against the University of Iowa, and I felt less apprehensive about flying and about visiting the Midwest.

During both games, our young team showed a lot of character. Everyone was gradually getting more excited for our season opener against USC. For me, it was an especially important game, because USC was a "hometown" school. I threw my all into practice that week. I wanted to perform at my very best in LA. By the time we got on the plane, I felt secure in the knowledge that our team was ready for the challenge.

Not long into the flight, my position coach got up and made his way down the aisle to my seat. He asked me to follow him and, of course, I did so, though I couldn't imagine what he wanted to talk about.

When we got to the rear of the plane, the coach told me the news: I would be starting against USC. This sent my head spinning. I wasn't sure what to think. This was in no way an expected development; there were at least two upperclassman "in line" ahead of me, and I had assumed it would be a long time before I started a game. I had expected to be eased into the line-up, playing a little bit here and there to get used to playing on the varsity team. Suddenly, I was starting against the University of Southern California, one of the best teams in the nation. I would be facing off against the likes of C.R. Roberts and Johnny Arnett. These were people who were the leading rushers in the nation, while I still felt like I was just getting my feet wet.

I didn't say any of this to the coach, of course.

Instead, I returned to my seat and stared out the window. When he told me about the change, I'd felt a little jolt of nerves—but afterward, looking out at the clouds, I felt my calm return. This information had not changed anything materially about the situation. We had still worked just as hard and prepared just as much, and I was still just as confident in the team.

We were playing in the Los Angeles Coliseum. As I ran out of the tunnel and onto the turf of the playing field, I had a moment of clarity: This is familiar territory for me. This was my city. I had played on this very spot as a high school student. This idea bolstered my confidence even more, and I was ready to give the game my very best.

Our young team (twenty-four sophomores, ten juniors, and seven seniors) took on this heavily favored Trojan team, and we had no fear of their huge front line or their very capable running backs, John Arnett and C.R. Roberts. Nevertheless, USC wound up beating us—but only just barely. In fact, newspaper coverage of the game declared it a "moral victory" for our team, because USC had been so heavily favored to win easily. Considering the challenge we'd faced, I felt good about our performance.

Once we were back in Oregon, the grind resumed, and the coaches didn't let up at all. We were back on the practice field and working harder than ever. We knew now that our next opponent would be ready for us—no more surprising teams who only knew the Oregon State team of old. Everyone had seen what we could do, and they'd throw everything they had at us. The coaches were pushing us hard, but we knew that it was necessary. I truly believe that we had the best coaching staff in college football at the time.

We were also hungry to really prove that we weren't the old Oregon State. The year before I arrived, the football team had only won one game their entire season. The guys on the team wanted to show everyone that those days were over and that we were going to perform at a much higher level.

Our next game was a tough matchup with Washington State University. It was a hard-fought game that we finally won, 24 to nothing. I even got a mention in the newspaper afterwards: "Earnel Durden, who weighed no more than 160 pounds when he stepped out of the shower, tallied three touchdowns for the Beavers."

Next up was UCLA. Of course, this was a special game for me. UCLA was a very good team and one of those expected to be in the running for a place in the Pasadena Rose Bowl. It was also the team I'd spent most of my youth watching and the team I had very nearly joined. UCLA was coming to us in Corvallis, and the symbolism of playing against this team I might have belonged to—on the home turf of the team I'd chosen instead—felt important.

The day of the game, I went to the upstairs dining room in the coliseum along with the rest of the team. It was raining, and I watched it pelt down as we ate together. After the meal was over, it was time for Coach Prothro to address the team.

It was very quiet, as it had been throughout the meal. Coach Prothro walked over to the window and slowly turned to face us.

"Men," he said, "I want you to know: The team that wins today is the team that wants it the most." And that was all he said.

Even for the notoriously tight-lipped coach, this was a laconic speech. My teammates and I knew what he was talking about, though. He was never one to shower us with praise or go into long pep talks. He kept things simple and direct. We were ready for this game; we knew that we were the ones who most wanted—even needed—the win. I had a great day. I averaged over fifteen yards for carry, on a rain-soaked field, and we beat UCLA 21 to 7.

The following week, we played UC Berkeley at Parker Stadium, on the Oregon State Campus, and we came back from a thirteen-point deficit to beat them, 21 to 13. We were riding pretty high on the waves of these successive wins, but our next opponent was poised to be our toughest yet.

We were set to play Stanford University down in Palo Alto. Chuck Taylor was the Stanford coach at the time—and a darn good one. He had assembled his team with care, hand-picking them with the goal of getting through the conference without a single loss. They were led by All-American quarterback John Brody, and they were a formidable prospect.

Before the game, I had a strange experience in the dining room where we were to have our pre-game meal. As soon as I walked in, I looked to the left and saw a large, flat board with our usual formation (balance-line single-wing) laid out in marshmallows, one marshmallow to represent each player in the starting line-up. Of course, someone had subbed in two small, chocolate marshmallows to represent Paul Lowe and myself. There was a message written next to the board indicating that we were no match for Stanford.

I didn't really know the genesis of this display. Was this something that someone had sent to the coaches? Was it something our coaches had cooked up themselves, to fire us up before the game? I also didn't entirely get the symbolism of the marshmallows. Was it to indicate that we were soft? Sweet? Good on a camping trip?

My marshmallow questions would not be answered, but the game itself was thrilling. John Brody demonstrated exactly why he led the nation in passing. By halftime, Stanford was leading, 19 to 7. As we had in the Berkeley game, we battled back in the second half, scoring one touchdown after another, and our defense kept Stanford off the board. The last touchdown came with a short-swing pass from Paul Lowe to me. I carried the ball fifty-nine yards to set up the winning touchdown, and we won the game by 20 to 19.

I spent the plane ride home running through the game in my mind, the way I did after nearly every game. When the plane landed in Corvallis, nothing seemed unusual. Buses were waiting to take us back to campus and we boarded them, mostly silent. Most of us were pretty tired or else still musing on the exciting game, so there wasn't much chatter. Then, when we reached campus, something unusual happened.

Instead of proceeding on its usual route, the bus drove over the curb and up onto the carefully manicured lawn in front of the student union. For a moment, I thought the bus driver had fallen asleep at the wheel, but he was awake and seemed cheerful. He opened the door for us, and the coaches ushered us out of the bus and into the student union, and then up onto a stage at the front of the room.

It seemed as though the entire student body was assembled before us. They were chanting and hollering and cheering for us. Through the cacophony, I began to make out words.

"WE WANT DURDEN! WE WANT DURDEN! WE WANT DURDEN!"

I felt my heart swelling. In that moment, I felt that I had finally come full circle. From feeling like the most ostracized outsider, I was now standing in front of my fellow students as they embraced and encouraged me. That single moment changed my perspective for the rest of my time at Oregon State.

I had another moment of personal significance around the same time, when Henry Ringer did a write-up of the Stanford game, saying:

"You can have USC's John Arnett, Michigan State's Clarence Peak, and all the rest of the All-American nominees—but Sanford University's Chuck Taylor will take Earnel Durden as 'one of the finest running backs I've ever seen.'"

That was huge for me, especially coming from Coach Taylor, who was one of the best coaches in the country and had worked with so many fine players. I felt I was really contributing to the team as a valued player, and I started to believe that Oregon State was on the verge of making history, coming back from a dismal recent past to have a hugely successful season.

The win in Palo Alto had put us on the cusp of the Rose Bowl, and we were all eager to make the cut. It seemed that my childhood dream was finally within my grasp. We had just two games remaining, against the University of Idaho and the University of Oregon. We had to win one of these games to officially throw our hat into the Rose Bowl ring, and we thought the University of Idaho was our best shot.

We practiced hard for the game against the University of Idaho, trying to anticipate anything the other team might bring to the field. What we hadn't prepared for was the weather. When we arrived in Moscow, Idaho, the town was certainly living up to its namesake, with the temperature a balmy zero degrees. As a Southern Californian boy, I had never experienced weather like this, let alone tried to play football in it.

That night, before I fell asleep, I legitimately wondered whether I was going to see the sun at all the next day.

It wasn't any warmer when we got up for breakfast. If anything, it felt colder! By game time, it was the coldest weather I'd ever experienced, and I'm sure many of the other guys on the team felt the same way. But we hadn't come here for a vacation—we had come here to solidify our chances at the Rose Bowl, and we weren't going to let anything stand in our way.

As the game started, I remember wading deep into the end zone for the kickoff. When the ball hit my hand, it felt like a rock crashing into me. I tucked it under my arm and started up the field. When I was tackled, it was as if someone had taken a bat to me. The cold amplified every painful or discomforting sensation. I knew this was going to be a brutal game.

The opposing team was also much better than I had realized. Their record after our matchup would demonstrate that. At least four players from that team went on to become NFL stars; the most famous were probably Jerry Cramer, who led the famed Green Bay Sweep to four Super Bowls, and Wayne Walker, who became an all-pro linebacker for the Detroit Lions. I often wondered how, with this caliber of players, Idaho consistently found itself in the bottom of the rankings.

With only a few minutes left in the game, Idaho was leading 10 to 7. Once again, our quarterback called my number in the huddle: he called wingback, out and down. We lined up in our left formation. The ball was snapped.

I broke down the field about six or seven yards, and then I

broke toward the sideline, keeping an eye on the cornerback all the way. When I saw the cornerback break hard toward me, I quickly started up the field. That way, the cornerback was out of position. Paul Lowe hit me with the short pass, the same pass we'd used to get fifty-nine yards against Stanford. This time, I went sixty-two yards, to the two-yard line.

Running out of time on the field, Paul Lowe scored on the fourth down, giving Oregon State the win, 14 to 10. That win secured Oregon State's place in the Rose Bowl.

When we got back home, the entire city of Corvallis was one big celebration. The streets were covered in rose petals, and everyone was in high spirits. It had been years since folks had a team to root for in the Rose Bowl, and they were delighted by the prospect.

As for me, I was preparing to make one of my most cherished childhood dreams a reality.

The 1957 Rose Bowl Team at our 50th Reunion (October 6, 2006). I am in the first row, second to the right.

CHAPTER FOUR

To the Rose Bowl and Beyond

Our path to the Rose Bowl wasn't clear, however. We still had to face the University of Oregon before heading to Pasadena to face off against Iowa. It wasn't just any game, either. The University of Oregon was our biggest rival, and we knew that they would give us a real fight.

Our coaches did not allow the looming Rose Bowl to distract us from training for the U of Oregon game. The team was glad for the extra practices—we all vowed that we weren't going to be caught short, as we had been against Idaho. By the time game day was upon us, we were feeling good about our chances.

We felt that we were ready. The University of Oregon team, however, had not been resting on their laurels all this time. The game quickly turned into a real knockdown, drag-out fight. Just before the half, I broke through the middle and started upfield. I was hit three, perhaps four times, but I stayed on my feet, only to finally be tackled on the five yard line, just before the gun went off and halftime officially began.

At the beginning of the third quarter, we kicked off to the University of Oregon. Just as I was getting in position to make the tackle, one of my teammates beat me to it. I picked myself up off the field and started back to our defensive huddle when I collided with one of their players. Not thinking much of the minor contact, I tried to go around him. To my surprise, he moved in front of me to prevent me from passing. I looked up at him, confused, and made a second attempt to get by. Once again, he stepped in front of me and blocked my path.

Earnel Durden carrying the ball, OSU vs. U of Oregon game

By this point, I'd had enough. Instead of trying to dart around him, I pushed him aside with both hands. Noticing this minor scuffle, officials ejected both of us from the game. I trudged over to the sidelines and sat down. On the other side of the field, I could see the opposing team, and they were behaving very strangely, jumping up and down in excitement as though they had won the game.

As we found out later, they had good reason to celebrate: Their ploy had worked. They had deliberately brought along a third-string guard and assigned him to annoy me until I did something that might get me removed from play.

I can't say for sure whether my absence from the game hurt us—I don't know how I would have performed. However, my replacement (an upperclassman) dropped two punts and was weak on the reverse. We wound up tying the game, and I can't help but think that those errors might have contributed to our final showing in the score.

The game with Oregon was a disappointment across the board—to the team, to the coaches and, most of all, to me. I couldn't shake feeling responsible for the tie. If only I hadn't been removed from the game, especially for what I thought was such a small infraction.

I knew, though, that I couldn't change the past. And it was hard to feel down for too long, with the Rose Bowl coming up. Eventually, sheer excitement muscled out the disappointment.

In contrast to the coaches' usual practice strategy, we had three days of light practices and an entire week off before we boarded the plane to Pasadena. The schedule gave us time to rest and re-center ourselves and, of course, to enjoy the atmosphere of celebration all over the town. It seemed that everyone was preparing for the game and cheering us on.

Finally, it came time to get on the plane to Los Angeles. The team was in high spirits for the entire flight. When we got off the plane, we were immediately bused to a hotel in Santa Monica, which we would call home during our time in LA.

We'd had a nice rest before we left Oregon, but now that we were in Los Angeles, the coaches didn't waste any time before plunging us back into football. There were meetings after meetings, an enormous amount of film study and, of course, double-day practices.

Our evenings, however, were a time for recreation. The team, most of whom had never been to Los Angeles, took advantage of the city. We took in shows and visited the famed logo at Lowry's on Restaurant Row. We had a whirlwind schedule. There always seemed to be somewhere we had to be, from *The Lawrence Welk Show* to an amusement park. It was sometimes difficult to go from a long day of grueling practice to an equally long night on the town, but it was a lot of fun, and we knew that it was a once-in-a-lifetime opportunity.

That idea bothered me increasingly as our time in LA went on. For most of these boys, this was the first and probably the last time they would see Los Angeles. For me, Los Angeles was simply home. I had always thought of it as a beautiful city, one of the world's greatest. But I was quickly realizing that, for all the years I had spent there, I didn't really know Los Angeles at all.

I grew up right there in the heart of city; my childhood homes were only about a forty-minute drive from the marvelous sights of Beverly Hills. Yet I knew only a fraction of what the city had to offer. I had never seen the amusement parks, the big studios, the fancy restaurants, and the grand hotels. I had watched TV every night without really realizing that those shows were filmed in my very own city.

It seemed to me that Los Angeles wasn't just one city, but rather a series of cities. I belonged to one Los Angeles and, for most of my life, I had rarely ventured out of it. Now I was standing in wings of TV studio, ready to be part of a live taping, and the feeling was overwhelming. I know the rest of my team was also excited, but it felt so much stranger for me. Virtually my entire childhood had been spent in Los Angeles, but it hadn't prepared me for any of this.

I vowed then and there that never again would I allow myself to be restricted to just a small portion of what my home city had to offer. I would revisit these places some day and embrace them as part of the full experience of this incredible place.

The Rose Bowl is traditionally played on New Year's Day, so naturally, part of our time in Los Angeles overlapped with Christmas. During that time, our schedules were relaxed slightly. Practices were shorter and we had fewer group meetings and not so many nighttime commitments.

Even with these allowances, spending the holidays in a hotel was very disorienting. It was especially strange for me because my family was so physically close. Virtually my entire family was a short car ride away, but I was not permitted to leave the hotel to spend Christmas with them. Coach Protho explained that it wouldn't be fair to let me go home to see my parents and siblings because my teammates did not have that option. Allowing just one or two players to do something special, because of an accident of geography, might lead to tensions with the others. Nevertheless, Coach Protho did extend an invitation to local families to visit us at the hotel, so even though it was an unorthodox situation, I did still get to see my family for Christmas.

Most of the other teammates had never been to LA in the winter and they were shocked at the mild weather. Used to brutal Oregon winters, they were dumbfounded by a sunny 85-degree Christmas Day.

Even while we were immersing ourselves in the city, we never forgot about the critical game that was inching closer each day. On game day, we awoke and ate a hearty breakfast before filing onto the bus for the twenty-mile trip to Pasadena. I was confident that the team was physically ready to play the game. But like the rest of the boys, I was very aware of the challenge before us.

Oregon State, Iowa Teams Wait Kickoff for Rose Bowl Game

Oregon State and Iowa Teams wait to kick off for Rose Bowl Game Starting 11 for each team (Earnel is in the top left corner.)

We were a young team, a lot of sophomores, and we would be facing a very mature team full of players who had been honing their skills longer than we had. We knew that differential might work against us, although we had beaten teams in the past who had older, more experienced players. Age was just one of dozens of factors that determined how a game of football might shake out.

The ride to Pasadena seemed to stretch out into an eternity. When we arrived at the Rose Bowl stadium, I sat down in front of my locker and went over and over my assignments, trying to engrave them on my brain. Eventually, I lay down on the floor and tried to simply clear my mind and just relax. It was much easier said than done.

My reverie was broken by the Special Teams Coach call for the centers, quarterbacks, punters, kickoff, and return people to get ready to take the field. I took refuge in the familiarity of these little pre-game rituals. No matter where we were or who we were playing or how important the game might be, there were certain chores we did before we stepped out on to any field. It grounded me to go through these motions and do things I'd done a hundred times before. The Rose Bowl may have been the culmination of a childhood dream, but it was also a game, and all games have certain commonalities.

Soon, the rest of the team joined us and we went through our pre-game warmups. After a while, the coach called us together. We gathered in the dressing room to make our final adjustments. As I had done before, the team stretched out on the floor, trying to find calm amidst the flutter of nerves and the thrill of anticipation. We waited there, still and silent, until it was time to take the field again.

It was strange how not strange it felt to walk out across the turf of the Rose Bowl stadium. As I stood on the five-yard line and waited for the game to begin, I looked up into the stands. It was an uncharacteristic move for me. Usually, I didn't pay any attention to the people in the stands. It wasn't that I didn't appreciate those who turned out to watch the game and cheer on the teams, but it wasn't something that I could afford to think much about when I had to focus on playing.

This time was different, however. The announcer had just informed us that the crowd that day numbered over 101,000. I looked up just to see what more than a hundred thousand people gathered together actually looked like. It looked vast, far larger than any other crowd I'd ever seen at one of my games.

I didn't have time to draw much of a conclusion from this because, at just that moment, I heard the official whistle. The game had begun.

I saw the ball heading toward me, twirling end of over end, almost as though it were in slow motion. I caught the ball and started up the field before being tackled somewhere around the 32-yard line. If I hadn't known it before, I was certain then that this would be a hard-fought game.

We weren't the only ones facing a challenge, however. We gave as good as we got, and both teams were scrapping hard for every point. With their huge front line and their big running backs, they gave us a very hard time on the ground game. Iowa was a very well-coached team, and their seniors were experienced and worked fluidly together and with the coaches. Our relative youth definitely put us at a disadvantage against them.

At some point in the game, I sustained what I thought was a minor injury. I was removed from play, but I expected to return shortly. The team doctor, however, did not agree with my assessment, and I was forced to sit out the rest of the game.

I watched the rest of the game from the sidelines as we pushed back against Iowa's skillful team. Eventually, they pulled out the win, but we didn't go down without a fight. Though the team was surely disappointed in the loss, it was still a fine showing for Oregon State. Each of us would have to manage our feelings about losing on our own, but we could all be proud of how hard we had worked and how vigorously we had fought.

I had mixed feelings about the experience on the whole, and it surprised me when we got off the bus back in Corvallis and were greeted by exuberant crowds cheering us on. They acted as though we had won the game and returned home conquering heroes. It occurred to me that, given the team's track record before the last year or two, we might as well have won. For the people of Corvallis, sending a team to the Rose Bowl was a victory in itself.

The game was a dramatic note to end my sophomore season upon, but I was pleased, on the whole, when I looked back on the year. For a young team with a rocky history, there was a lot to be proud of in that year, and I felt there was a lot of promise for seasons to come. Thinking about the future and what it might hold for our team took some of the sting out of the Rose Bowl loss.

As the season was wrapping up, accolades from state and national bodies began rolling in for individual players. The one that really caught my eye was the UCLA All-Opponent team. Every year, UCLA would select one player from each team—someone who had performed well in a game against them—and they would bring that player back for a gala celebration. That year, I had the honor of being selected to represent Oregon State University. I was delighted by the prospect.

Part of the UCLA All-Opponent team, 1956. I am in the top row, on the right. (The girl in the middle starred in the motion picture "The Bad Seed"!)

We were put up in the Beverly Hills Hotel and catered to like kings. On the night of the gala, each player was introduced individually with a little speech about how they had played against the Bruins the prior year. It was an incredible feeling to be distinguished for my individual efforts as a player, but the social aspect was even more enjoyable.

The UCLA All-Opponent team on stage at the Beverly Hills Hotel, receiving our awards (1956). I am the fourth person in from the far left.

The atmosphere was convivial and fun. Finally, I had the chance to really meet and interact with players I had only encountered on the football field. Naturally, we shared a lot of the same interests, and we were able to really get a sense of one another as people, rather than just opponents.

The gala was a nice break from regular life, but soon I was back on campus, attending classes and preparing for exams. After the football season ended, I was able to put most of my focus on my schoolwork and that was, for the most part, how I spent my time.

Every year at Oregon State there was a contest to elect a "typ-ical" sophomore student, one girl (called "Betty Co-Ed") and one boy (called "Joe College"). The idea was that these individuals would most fully embody the college experience at Oregon State. I didn't pay much attention to this contest, despite being a soph-omore, but I did know that each house on campus (sixty-four in total) would put forth one member for the entire student body to vote upon.

My candidacy began as a joke. Even before the contest, my housemates had called me "Joe College" in fun. It was true that, on the surface, I was far from the "typical" student, being very ob-viously not White in an incredibly White place. But the joke also worked because I did so many of the "Joe College" things. I played sports, focused on studies, and developed a rapport with my house-mates. Like the best jokes, it was funny because it was a bit true. I sort of was a "Joe College," just with a slightly different face than people were used to seeing.

So when someone submitted my name for the contest, we all had a good laugh. But then the first round of voting came and went, reducing the pool from sixty-four to forty, and my name was still there. The next round took it down to twenty-four names, and mine was still amongst them. A third round took the race down to just twelve names, including mine. Then it started to become less a joke and more a serious campaign.

Around our house, it was considered a matter of pride—it would be a feather in all of our caps to have a house member voted Joe College! The guys all turned out to try to scrape up votes for me; it seemed that the whole house was supporting me. The pool of names just kept shrinking with every round of voting, twelve to six, six to three. My name was still there.

The three Joe College finalists, from left to right: Socolosky, Durden, and McKennon

The final votes would be cast and the winners announced after a big dance in the Coliseum. The dance was great fun, and at the end of the night came the big announcement. The final vote, which had taken place during the dance, had determined that I was, in fact, Joe College—the epitome of what a male sophomore should be, according to the tradition.

The honor felt somewhat bewildering to me, as someone who had struggled with belonging and acceptance. I so often felt different, like an outsider. Being declared "usual," "typical," even "normal" was huge for me. It made an immeasurable difference to my self-confidence. I was able to move through the world more assured, ready to face the challenges that lay before me. Even my classes seemed less difficult. I felt more and more like I belonged on campus, like it was a home for me.

Every year on Mother's Day, students invited their mothers to visit the campus and see what daily life was like for their youngsters. That year, I was more eager than ever to show my mother the life I had built in Oregon. It took a little cajoling, but I finally got my mother to agree to visit me.

Los Angeles to Corvallis by bus was nearly a twenty-four hour trip, so it was a bit of a trek for her. Naturally, I met her at the bus depot and gave her a short tour of the campus and the town. I was so excited to show my mother these parts of my life that she had never seen before and, as it turned out, my mother was very popular with the other mothers.

It seemed that everyone wanted to meet my mom and quiz her about our family, about what it was like watching me play on Saturdays, and how she had felt about the Rose Bowl. Nearly everywhere we went, someone would stop us to chat. What the eager mothers who stopped to visit with her didn't know, however, was that my mother had rarely seen me play a game of football. While she was incredibly proud of me, she couldn't stand to watch the brutal tackles that I sometimes received on the field. For her, it was just too difficult to watch her son seemingly being hurt.

She did start watching more games after I explained to her that I didn't really feel all of the hits. Between the padding and the adrenaline, most of the tackles looked a lot worse than they actually felt. That eased her mind somewhat, but I don't think she ever really grew accustomed to seeing her child forcefully driven into the ground.

Coincidentally, that weekend, most of the small shops downtown had decorated the figures and mannequins with my number! It was something they occasionally did to show pride in various players, and I was glad that my mother was able to see the city supporting me.

I could tell that my mother was very proud of me and what I had accomplished, and seeing that pride made me happier than I can say. My mother had supported me through the uncertainty of college selection and the long, strange adjustment period in Oregon. She had always been there for me and had nurtured my ambitions and my goals. I felt like I finally had something to show for her hard work and her faith in me. It felt so good to be able to make her proud.

When I escorted her back to the bus that would take her home to Los Angeles, we both knew that this weekend would loom large in our memories. She seemed so happy. Knowing how she had sacrificed and saved and worked throughout my childhood, I couldn't think of any greater gift to offer her.

Spring faded into summer and I returned to Los Angeles, spending some important quality time with my family. I worked again, but I also made time for old friends as well as for June and her family. I even returned to Jordan-Downs, where many of my friends remained. They had graduated from high school but, for most of them, nothing else had changed.

I was happy to see them and they seemed happy to see me as well. They told me they had followed my career and said how proud they were of me. Being back there was a strange experience, however. I felt like I was returning from the moon rather than Oregon. The physical distance between us wasn't so great, but suddenly it seemed as though millions of miles and dozens of years had passed.

A few of my friends had gone to college locally, and some had enrolled in trade schools in the area. Very few of them had continued with athletics at the college level, which was understandable. College is hard, and it's even harder if you come from a working class background. Many of my peers needed to keep a job (or jobs) as well as complete their studies. It was no surprise that they didn't have time for the rigors of a major sport.

I knew that my path wasn't for everyone, but I was delighted that so many of my peers had attended some form of higher education. As I made my own way through college, it became increasingly clear to me how important education was, especially for young African-American men and women. Whether it was vocational training or an Ivy League school, attending some sort of institution of higher learning was an important step toward success in an often-hostile world.

My friends and acquaintances who didn't take that next step and lacked the structure of continuing education seemed to be at loose ends. Many of the problems they had were problems that are still plaguing young people today, especially in the Black community. I know that attending college is often very difficult, especially for students from rough backgrounds, but I truly feel that it's one of the best and surest ways to make one's way in the world. It gives shape to a young life, pushes students toward goals, and encourages them to think beyond the limitations of the places where they grew up.

I knew as I drove away from Jordan-Downs that day that I had transcended my early life. Everything might have started right here in this housing project, but I knew that my life had expanded so far beyond the little world that might have been, a place bounded on all sides by poverty, inequality, and violence.

It was hard that summer to say goodbye to my family, my mother and stepfather and my brothers and sister, but I felt a sense of peace about returning to Oregon that I hadn't experienced before. I had learned that, sometimes, I would have to push through unpleasant experiences and come out the other side into something better, something worth the pain or discomfort. I would never relish leaving my family, friends, and city behind me, but I had also developed another life—a good life—at college.

It was a long drive back to Corvallis, but there was something fine and important waiting at the other end.

CHAPTER FIVE

A Career Cut Short

Soon I was back on campus getting ready for the double-day practices that always characterized the beginning of the pre-season. I had heard Coach Prothro say that this was a team that should have been in the Rose Bowl. We had been so young and relatively inexperienced—only three games of freshman experience—the previous year when we had faced off against Iowa in Pasadena. Coach Prothro, among others, felt that if we'd had a little more time and a few more games under our belts, we might have had a different outcome.

My junior year, the team had thirty-one returning players comprised of twenty-four juniors and seven seniors. Now, in addition to our existing skill set, we were seasoned and battle-tested. Everyone was expecting a lot from the new and improved Oregon State team that year, myself included.

We opened our season against USC and Portland at Multnomah Stadium (these days known as Providence Park). Many spectators and analysts believed that our team and USC represented the two most competitive teams in the conference. One paper even suggested that: "This single game, matching the conference's two top, pre-season choices, could decide the conference championship on the very first weekend."

The question became, what was in it for Oregon State University? After all, we knew we couldn't return to the Rose Bowl; at the time, there was a no-repeat clause, which meant that a team couldn't play in the Rose Bowl for two consecutive seasons. The answer was simple: Oregon State hadn't beaten USC since 1946. At that point, USC was the only California team that hadn't been beaten by a Prothro-coached team—and after our near miss with them the previous season, we felt we were closer than ever to changing that.

Anticipation was high as the game approached. Not only was this our first outing of the season and a chance to announce ourselves as the new, more mature team we had become, but it was also potentially a historic match. USC was well prepared, as always.

Nevertheless, every time they came close to scoring, our defense would rise up to put them down. We finally beat the tough USC team 21 to nothing, and the 100-mile ride back to Corvallis was filled with celebration.

The following week, we headed out to play the University of Kansas. At the time, there was a fairly popular song called "I'm Going to Kansas City" by Wilbert Harrison. One portion of the lyrics goes:

> *I'll be standing on the corner*
> *On the corner of Fifth Street and Vine*
> *I'm gonna be standing on the corner*
> *On the corner of Fifth Street and Vine*
> *With my Kansas City baby*
> *And a bottle of Kansas City wine.*

I got together with a few of the players and we vowed that we were going to stand "on the corner of Fifth Street and Vine," just as the song said. During some of our down time in the city, we did indeed hunt out that very corner, ensuring that we would have a tale to tell our friends when we got back to Oregon. Next to the game itself, that was easily the highlight of the trip.

After the game, the papers declared that: "Kansas City couldn't solve Durden and his speed. Two of his fast reverses, slippery running in the open, and 63-yard and 35-yard drives rapidly became first-quarter touchdowns."

We went on to beat University of Kansas 34 to 6 and, the following week, we were off to Dyche Stadium in Evanston, Illinois, to play Northwestern University. More than 34,500 fans turned out to watch as we beat Northwestern 22 to 13. I had a great game, making 32 yards of a 58-yard drive in the final period. We were all riding high after three victories in a row.

The next week, we beat the University of Idaho, 20 to nothing. We all felt that we were fulfilling Coach Prothro's words from the start of the season about how we were, truly a team at the top of our powers.

We encountered some trouble, however, in our next game against the UCLA Bruins. The previous year, we had beaten them at Oregon State University on a rain-soaked field. Now, we would be flying down to LA to play at the Coliseum; this game would be on UCLA's turf, and they were ready for us.

There weren't many teams who had beaten a UCLA team coached by Red Sanders, let alone two seasons in a row. We knew that the Bruins would be particularly eager to keep us from pulling out another win. At the UCLA All-Opponent Team Gala, I'd had the chance to meet Coach Sanders. He had complimented me on the fine job both the team and I had done against UCLA in Corvallis. I was very proud of that game, having averaged fifteen yards per carry in that game and shredding UCLA's defense on kickoff and punt returns.

Coach Sanders told me something else as well, which I reflected upon as we prepared to take the field in Los Angeles: "Earnel, I brought that balance-line single wing to the West Coast and I know how to stop it."

At the time, it was just a light, passing comment. We had been enjoying the celebration's convivial atmosphere, so his words hadn't seemed aggressive. As we prepared to face the Bruins once again, however, I couldn't help but wonder if the coach's remark had been a sort of warning.

The game was actually billed as the "Battle of the Single Wings." At the time, there were only three teams in the nation using that offense: Oregon State, Tennessee, and UCLA. Coach Sanders had indeed brought the strategy from Tennessee, and Coach Prothro, in turn, had taken it to Oregon State.

It was UCLA who finally broke our winning streak, beating us 26 to 7. It was an incredibly tough game, and the Bruins really made us fight. By this time in our season, my team had gotten used to winning, and this loss was tough to swallow. We flew home feeling deflated.

As I sat on the plane, I found myself coming back to Coach Sanders's words, which now seemed to have been prophetic. I wondered what he had done to get around the previously unbeatable single-wing. I was eager to get back to Corvallis so I could examine the film of the game, which the team always watched. Seeing ourselves in action allowed us to understand what had happened in the game on a micro level, instead of just from our individual perspectives, and it allowed us to refine our techniques, both individually and as a team.

After going over the game tapes again and again, I realized that Coach Sanders had indeed come up with a way to contain my reverse, thus seriously limiting our attacks. As I watched, I hoped that other teams had not picked up on this weakness in our strategy.

Being a more experienced team was a plus, in general, but it did mean that our opponents had more opportunities to study us and figure out what made our plays work. From now on, it would be very difficult for us to "surprise" an opponent.

The following week, it was the University of Washington at Seattle, and the beautiful weather brought out the crowds. Washington was ready for us—more proof that we weren't going to sneak by anyone this year. Washington scored first. Our defense rose up and stopped them time and time again, but it proved too little, too late. Washington won the game 17 to 6.

This was devastating for the entire team—our second loss in as many weeks. I was sure that University of Washington had done their homework and that they had copied UCLA's attack against us.

After two weeks of disappointing defeats, our coaches pushed us to really throw ourselves into practices. We were spending so much time in practice that I found it difficult to balance studying with my increasingly time-consuming commitment to football. Though I was physically drained most days, I stayed up late studying, because I knew that my grades were just as important as what I was doing on the football field.

It was a home game the next week against Washington State. After two straight losses, we needed to win this game. I was feeling good, headed into the game. For some reason, I always played my best games against two teams: Stanford University and Washington State. I could never figure out exactly why that was, but I was looking forward to putting the theory to the test.

My fellow teammates and my coaches shared a similar sentiment—I could sense that we were deeply confident and very ready for this matchup. We had taken our licks in recent weeks, but then we had stepped up practice and really honed our skills. We were ready to get back to winning.

Beavers Dump Golden Bears·

OREGON STATE WINGBACK Earnel Durden packs the pigskin for a short gain in the Beavers winning touchdown march. The Beavers rallied in the second half of their ball game Saturday to overcome a 13-0 deficit and win by a score of 21-to-13. The Beaver ground attack marched their way to three touchdowns in the second half and the OSC defense bottled up the Cal passing attack that carried Cal to an early lead. The onrushing Bears shown closing in on Durden are Joe Kapp (22), Don Gilkey (61), and Bill Vallotton (80). (photo by Glen Lee.)

Newspaper clipping from one of my Oregon State vs. University of California games (before my injury)

He's Dependable Sophomore

Earnel Durden, Oregon State's fine sophomore wingback, may get chance to ramble Saturday against Washington State college. Durden has been steady work-horse, averaging better than five yards per carry.

Newspaper clipping from Oregon State vs. Washington State game

PASADENA, HERE WE COME! DURDEN SETS SAIL

PHOMORE WINGBACK Earnel Durden (14) takes advantage of some e blocks to pick up yardage in the opening minutes of Saturday's game with Stanford at Palo Alto. Minutes later OSC scored the first touchdown. Beaver protectors are Terry Salisbury (80), and Bob DeGrant (88). (UP)

Newspaper clipping from one of my Oregon State vs. Stanford games (before my injury)

We played a good game against Washington State and, once again, I was having a great day on the field. Our offense was moving the ball well and our defense was, for the most part, stopping Washington State at every turn.

Then, late in the fourth quarter, I took the ball on a wingback reverse. As I started up the field, I was tackled from the left side. It felt to me like the kind of hit I'd taken a thousand times before. When I stood up, however, I realized that something was different. As I walked back to our huddle, I suddenly felt a sharp, excruciating pain around my knee.

Every athlete is wary of injury, and I knew when I felt that stabbing pain that I had to take myself out of the game and consult with the trainer. He gave my knee a cursory inspection and wrapped it in ice. I felt better almost immediately and, after a short rest, I told the coaches that I was ready to re-enter the game.

I joined the team on the field but, after only two or three plays, my knee began to swell visibly. The pain came back, as strong—or stronger—than before. I removed myself from the game again and went to the trainer, who examined the knee in more detail. He wrapped it in ice again, but this time, he also summoned the team doctor to offer his opinion.

The doctor gave my knee a brief examination before declaring that it was not very serious, which was a huge relief for me. We went on to beat Washington State 39 to 25 and, as far as I was concerned, my knee injury was just a footnote to an otherwise incredible game.

Almost as soon as I returned back to the dorms however, it became clear that my injury wasn't just going to go away. We were gearing up for University of California and practicing hard. It was especially difficult for me because of the pain and swelling I was still experiencing in my leg. After each practice, I would ice my knee until the swelling went down. Of course, a few hours later, the swelling would return and I would have to begin the cycle all over again.

The swelling eventually started increasing, no matter what I did. It was alarming and frustrating, and eventually the coaches stepped in. They put me on the "Injury Reserve" list, which meant no practices and no games until I had a clean bill of health. Our team went on to beat Cal, 21 to 19, but I remained on the injured list for the rest of the season.

Though I couldn't play in the games, I watched as our team beat Stanford (24 to 14) and finished the season strong with a 10 to 7 win over University of Oregon. We finished out the season with a very respectable 8–2 record. It would have been good enough to send us back to the Rose Bowl, if we had been eligible.

It was disappointing not to be able to get out on the field and play with my teammates, but I was still incredibly proud of the great work my fellow players were doing. Plus, I assumed that my stay on the injured list would be brief. I believed my knee had only minor problems, which could easily be alleviated with rest and recovery.

During the off-season, the coaches took me back to the team's doctor, who confirmed this hypothesis. He suggested I simply rest the knee for a while and said it would heal itself. The team trainer kept putting ice on the knee, and my injured joint went through the now-familiar cycle of swelling, receding slightly, and then swelling again.

I couldn't help but notice that, no matter how much I iced my knee and no matter how much I rested it, there wasn't any noticeable improvement. In fact, the injury actually seemed to be getting worse, rather than better. Eventually, it became so painful that I couldn't walk without limping.

By the time spring practice started, I found myself completely unable to participate, even in a limited way. Finally, Coach Prothro told me he was sending me to Portland to see a specialist. I was hoping that this expert could tell me what was going on with my knee and give me a concrete fix, but I also was worried that I might require surgery. As it turned out, it was much worse than that.

Even today, I remember my conversation with the specialist in perfect detail. I remember the art prints on the wall; I remember how he parted his hair and the tie he wore as he said to me: "I don't think that you will ever play football again."

It was all the more devastating for being so unexpected. After months of assurances from the team doctor, I was expecting to hear that I would, at worst, have a long recovery time ahead of me. Nothing had prepared me for the idea that my football career might be over.

Almost immediately, my mind flitted back to the team doctor and the numerous times he had reassured me that my knee had suffered no major damage. I couldn't help but wonder if the months

I had spent essentially ignoring my injury and having no real medical treatment had exacerbated what might have originally been a fixable problem. Had the team doctor's misdiagnosis robbed me of a football career?

I wasn't the only person who was shocked by this information. Coach Prothro was surprised and furious. We both couldn't believe that the team doctor had been so dismissive of what had turned out to be a grave injury. I wasn't there when Coach Prothro confronted the team doctor with the news from the specialist, but I heard that it was not a pleasant conversation.

Even though the specialist had been very frank with me, I wasn't ready to face the reality of my situation. Instead, I convinced myself that if I just got into the weight room and really worked on my knee, I could recover and play once again. The specialist told me that my knee did indeed require surgery, but I actually saw that as a positive. Surely, once I had my knee fixed medically, it just be a matter of finding the right exercise regimen to get back into fighting shape.

The trainer scheduled my surgery around finals week. I took three of my final exams and made arrangements with my professors to take the other two when I returned. The surgery was performed in the specialist's hospital up in Portland. I spent three days in recovery before the trainer drove up to bring me back to campus.

My family, obviously, could not be there for the surgery, but they were the first thing I thought about afterwards. As soon as I got back to campus, I wanted to get away. I wanted to go to my home and see my loved ones.

Right away, I got in contact with my professors and took my remaining finals before going back to Heckart Lodge to pack. I was moving slowly and on crutches, but I loaded up the car as quickly as I could, setting out for LA around five o'clock in the evening.

Once I got on the road, I didn't stop for anything but gas. My knee throbbed; the pain was even more acute after the surgery. I had been prescribed some pain pills at the hospital, but I knew I couldn't take them while I was driving. I was already tired when I started out, and I drove all through the night, keeping all the windows rolled down in the hope that the cold night air would keep me awake.

It was not the most pleasant journey I had ever taken. It wasn't even the most pleasant version of that particular journey (Corvallis to LA) I had ever taken. But I was focused and single-minded. All I could think about was getting home to my family. With that clear goal in mind, it seemed that everything else faded into the background. My anxiety over my football career, my frustration at how the situation had turned out, my sadness over the potential loss of something I loved—all of it was forced to the back of my mind.

I drove a full night and day without sleeping. The pain in my leg was unending. Finally, when I thought I could not go on, I glimpsed the beautiful Sierra Pelona Mountains, visible from the Ridge Route. I knew from previous experience that this meant I was approaching the outskirts of LA. I would just have to cross the mountains and I would be back in my city. I was nearly home. The sight of those mountains, and the nearness to my family that they represented, gave me a much-needed burst of energy in the final stretch.

Just before I reached the mountains themselves, I stopped at a gas station to wash my face and compose myself. For a moment, I had almost forgotten about my knee. The pain never went away, but like anything constant and regular, I had started to acclimate to it.

I had no physical resources left at that point. I was exhausted, I was suffering, and the only thing that pushed me onwards was my knowledge that I was so close to my destination. It was mind over matter. I felt that now, more than ever, I had to prove to myself that my mind—my will—was stronger than any amount of pain. I threw my crutches in the back seat and climbed into the driver's seat. I was too close to home to let anything get in my way.

When I was coming down the back side of the mountain into the greater LA area, I kept the windows down and I sang loudly to myself to stay awake. Soon, I found myself on the Harbor Freeway, just a few miles from my home. As I pulled up in front of my house, I saw my mom already waiting for me in the doorway.

I was so exhausted that I could barely make it inside the house. I can't imagine what I looked like to her, awkwardly staggering on crutches like a sickly old man. The trip to Los Angeles from Corvallis was usually about twenty-four hours on the team bus. I had made it in just eighteen hours, and I certainly was the worse for wear. My mother must have seen the pain and the exhaustion in my face, because she didn't ask me to explain anything. Instead, I had just enough energy to greet my family before I retired to my bedroom and slept for as long as I could manage.

My knee woke me, some hours before I wanted to be awake, and I was finally able to take my pain medication, safe in my family's home. The medication did help slightly, but I knew that my struggle was far from over. I didn't just have to rebuild my leg (to whatever degree that was even possible). I also had to re-evaluate myself as a person and an athlete. The future was full of uncertainty. I had no idea how strong my leg would be or how difficult it would be to cope with my new limitations. It was shaping up to be a long, hard summer.

Over those months, I kept the coaches apprised of my progress. They had set me up with some doctors in Los Angeles and I also made sure that those medical professionals knew what was happening at every stage in my recovery. I wasn't going to make the mistake of ignoring my injury again.

I started a slow and moderate exercise program for my knee. Eventually, I was able to get to the point where I no longer needed my crutches to get around. I still believed that, with the proper rehabilitation, I would play football again. So when I set about re-training my knee, I exercised carefully and in increments, because I knew that everything I did now would determine my long-term recovery.

As the pain gradually became more manageable, I stepped up my exercise regime. Every day, it seemed more and more likely that I might return to the football team—at least as far as I was concerned. But I had become so accustomed to my knee in its worst, most destroyed condition that I'd forgotten how much I had previously been able to do and just how punishing football really was on the body. I had come a long way since the surgery, but I still wasn't anywhere near capable of taking the kind of hits I'd once shrugged off easily.

Although I had gone through each step in my recovery meticulously, I still just didn't have the strength in that leg to be competitive on the football field. No matter how much I hoped or wished or worked or trained, I couldn't completely fix my broken body. My leg was not unlike a hastily broken plate. No matter how patient or skilled the repair, the cracks would always show, and the plate would always be weaker in those places.

The truth was staring me right in the face, but I just wasn't ready to open up my eyes.

It was clear even to me, however, that I would never play college football again. When I went back to Oregon State in the fall, I would be entering my senior year and, for all my painful progress over the summer, my leg just wasn't going to be ready by then. I would miss out on my last year of college football, for sure, but I still had hopes of possibly playing at the professional level. I thought if I could rehabilitate my leg over the course of the school year, I could come back for the pro season after I graduated.

I met with Coach Prothro and asked him about this plan. He

suggested I take it slow and steady and keep working on my knee. Over the course of the year, we would evaluate my progress and determine how far I might be able to go.

Before my injury, going out for a professional football team had been a foregone conclusion. I expected to get some interest from various teams and, indeed, now that I was a senior, a number of teams were sending letters. It seemed like every team in the league was expressing interest in me—but the most persistent, by far, were the Green Bay Packers. They even sent two scouts out to meet with me and examine my knee. Similarly, the Saskatchewan Rough Riders (as the name suggests, they were a team in the Canadian Football League) sent representatives to check out my recovery.

Pro teams were still interested in me, even with the injured leg—but it was also clear that the knee and my recovery would absolutely be a factor in their decisions about me.

Fall was also the time of year when the All-Star games (the Senior Bowl and the Hula Bowl) were prepared. These games were designed to allow graduating seniors to showcase their talents for professional scouts. Any player who was serious about going into the national football leagues wanted to play in one of those games.

Stanford's coach, Chuck Taylor, came to Coach Prothro and asked how I was doing and whether he thought that my knee would be ready in time for the Hula Bowl, because he wanted to include me on his roster. It was a great honor and would have been a very exciting opportunity, but reality tempered my happiness when Coach Prothro called me into his office to discuss the idea. We talked for a long time and we both finally agreed that my knee would not be strong enough to go through the rigors of practice and a demanding All-Star game. Even if I didn't hurt my knee further, there was no way that I would be able to perform up to my usual standards, let alone impress any scouts.

This was a bitter pill to swallow—or rather, a series of bitter pills.

As the fall wore on, it became increasingly clear that my chances of playing professional football were dwindling. Not only would I be unable to play for my final year, but I also wasn't strong enough to show scouts the skills that had interested them in the first place.

I had decided long ago that football was going to be my life, one way or another. Now, with my future uncertain, I had to think seriously about backup plans. Though I certainly hoped that I would regain normal function in my leg, I couldn't rely on that. By extension, I couldn't rely on being drafted for an NFL team. If I ever had that opportunity, I would absolutely take it. But in the meantime, I had to figure out how to make a living and stay connected to the game that I loved.

During spring practice that year, I spent a lot of time on the sidelines watching the young players do their drills. It was an entirely new perspective on the game, and it felt a little like an out-of-body experience, watching new players learn the plays and techniques I'd used a thousand times before.

That feeling was especially pronounced when I watched the backs finding their rhythm and learning to run the reverse. The reverse was my play; it felt as though it had been made for me and, over the course of my career, I had run it to perfection.

The reverse, which had been a critical part of our overall attack strategy, was built on precision timing. The wingback had to start the reverse two seconds before the ball was snapped, and the ball had to hit the tailback's hands at the exact moment that the wingback arrived. Then the fullback and tailback could feint, temporarily hiding the ball. Before the other team even realized it, the wingback would have sprung either inside or outside of their defense. When it worked perfectly, it was like a magic trick and, over the years, my team had learned how to run it like clockwork.

The coaches had so much faith in this play that they sometimes ran it when we were down on the ten-yard line. Watching the newbies going through the motions, I wondered if it was actually the play that made them so confident or if it was me. Letting go of the idea of playing football wasn't just one terrible realization, it was a series of tiny losses, like that one. When I understood that I couldn't run the reverse anymore, one more piece of the identity I had built for myself was gone.

Even while I was experiencing the painful process of watching the team go on without me, I was also realizing what an important education I had been getting all along. Of course, I had noticed the coaching of the team when I was a player. But being outside the game allowed me to really see the over-arching strategy in what Coach Prothro and his assistant coaches were doing.

I watched closely as the coaches split the players into small groups to maximize their teaching. This was something that set a Prothro-coached team apart from everyone else: individualized instruction. As a player, I had never given much thought to what the other players were doing or how they were being taught. I had been totally focused on making sure that I was doing what was needed to help the team succeed. Now I could see how hard the coaches worked to tailor their instruction to different players and different positions. They had to see the whole picture and keep it in their heads at all times, even when they were working with just one individual.

I also appreciated the coaches' attention to technique. I watched our linemen being taught to bend their knees and keep a wide stance when blocking, to strike upwards through their opponents, and to always keep their feet moving. I remembered my own instruction as a punt returner: I was told to find the ball off the kicker's foot, go to where the ball is going to come down, settle in and catch the ball, locking it into my hands. From the outside looking in, I could appreciate the rock-solid base the coaching had given us players. It was something that not all players received. Even today, if you watch a football game on television, there's a good chance you will see a player catching the punt on the run or over his shoulders, thus creating opportunities for fumble.

In addition to the technical skills of football, our coaches were just as adept at dealing with the emotional and mental elements of the game. Some might imagine that, because Coach Prothro was a low-key and relatively quiet man, he couldn't whip us into a frenzy with one of those booming speeches that you see in football movies. It was true that Coach Prothro wasn't a "fire and brimstone" coach. He was never going to get up in front of us and thunder about destiny and tenacity. But the effects of those big, theatrical speeches only last about five or ten minutes into a game. All too often, a big speech contains little actual wisdom—it's just platitudes shouted in an exciting way. A speech like that is good for a quick burst of energy, but it has no staying power.

Instead, Coach Prothro worked all the time to instill confidence in the players, which was part of his coaching technique. He didn't expect one speech to win a game. He put in the hours before and after games, at practices, and during the off-season to make sure we felt ready and strong. We didn't need one big speech, because we had a thousand small conversations that bolstered our confidence and made us feel prepared.

As I observed more practices, I realized that my coaches had not only taught me how to be a better player, but they had also provided an excellent example for how to be an outstanding coach. In my mind, Oregon State had the best coaching staff around. I realized that everything I needed to know about coaching was right in front of me. I'd been surrounded by it since I arrived on campus.

At the same time, I was also realizing that, if I couldn't play football, then coaching might be the best way for me to stay close to the game. I felt that I could be a good coach—after all, I'd had excellent examples. Coaching was something I could actively pursue without having to wait for my leg to recover.

As soon as I realized what I wanted to do, I started working toward a career in coaching. Every year, Oregon State held a job fair where they would invite various companies to come to campus and visit with our seniors. During these weeks, the campus would be packed with representatives from all sorts of industries interviewing soon-to-be graduates for potential job opportunities.

I made sure to make myself available for these job fairs and to express my interest in coaching. I also let Coach Prothro know about my plans, because he obviously had a great deal of insight into what coaching required and how to get started. Coach Prothro was happy to advise and, when asked about students who might be interested in coaching football, he was more than willing to drop my name.

During the job fair, a representative approached Coach Prothro from a large school district in the San Bernadino/Riverside area. He apparently asked Coach Prothro a bit about me and indicated that I was exactly what he was looking for.

Finally, the representative approached me and asked if we could talk about the prospect of my coaching in one of their high schools. I was elated, though I tried to keep a neutral expression. He was talking about a Head Coach position at a large high school, which was exactly what I wanted. We had a very good chat, and he seemed interested in me as a candidate. When he left, he told me he would get back in touch with me in a couple of weeks.

The whole tenor of the meeting and his statements had led me to believe that a job offer was imminent. I even wrote to my mother to tell her about the incredible opportunity and how excited I was. It seemed that all I had to do now was wait, and that's exactly what I did.

A couple of weeks went by, and then a couple more. Soon, it had been more than a month without any word from the school representative. Finally, I went to Coach Prothro to ask what had happened, assuming that he would have more information than I did.

Coach Prothro seemed surprised that I hadn't heard anything yet, and he agreed to check on the situation for me. In a few days, Coach Prothro called me into his office. By then, I was expecting that the job offer had fallen through in some way, but I wasn't prepared for what he told me:

"The school district wasn't ready for a Black coach," he said.

I just sort of froze up for a moment. It felt like my heart had stopped beating. I just stood there, silent, before slowly turning and walking out of the office. Racism was like this, I realized. It burst into your life when it was least expected, when you felt safe and respected, and it slapped you in the face with the idea that some people would always think of you as lesser.

I thought back over the interview obsessively. He had come after me, I thought. He knew who I was when he approached me. I had never tried to hide my race—I wouldn't have, even if I could. Why was my race now a factor in this decision? One of the most frustrating things about racism is how inexplicable it is. I knew that I would never get an answer to these questions, because there was no good answer.

It took me a long time to put that disappointment behind me, but I knew that I couldn't dwell on it forever. I still needed a job after graduation, and if I wanted to be a coach in a school somewhere, I needed to make sure that all of my i's were dotted and t's were crossed.

I had loaded up on required courses earlier in my college career and so, by the beginning of my third quarter senior year, I only had my student teaching left to complete. The university made arrangements for me to do my student teaching at Jefferson High

School in Portland. I have always wondered about that decision, as there were a number of other school districts much closer, and other student teachers were stationed much closer to the college. Perhaps some of the smaller local towns were also "not ready" for a Black teacher—even a student teacher? Or perhaps it was simple academic bureaucracy. I didn't dig into the issue too deeply because I was actually happier going to Portland, a larger city with more to interest a young person.

My professors arranged to come to Portland once or twice per month. They were there to check on me, but I was sure they also had frequent meetings with my supervising teacher, Tom Silva. He was a great friend and mentor. Like me, he was a former football player and graduate of Oregon State. I appreciated his experience and his integrity.

That year, Jefferson's football team had won the state championship, due in no small part to great coaching (along with some excellent players). Student teaching there was the ideal experience for anyone who wanted to be a coach. I got to see young men like Terry Baker (who would go on to become Oregon State's only Heisman trophy winner) and Mel Renfro (who would play for the Dallas Cowboys for many years and became an All-Pro defensive back) early in their careers.

In Portland, I made arrangements to live with an elderly family by the name of Leftridge. Mr. Leftridge worked as a union organizer alongside people like Phillip Randolph. He helped to develop the Brotherhood of Sleeping Car Porters, one of the first primarily Black unions in the United States. He was working to make this happen during the time that I stayed with him, and it wasn't until I returned to LA and talked with some friends that I found out he had met his goals—and made history at the same time.

As both of the Leftridges were getting on in years, it was nice for them to have a young person around the house. They owned a brand new Buick, which neither of them could drive anymore, so I would take them to church every Sunday and around to other errands. It was a good arrangement for all of us. I enjoyed staying with them, and they enjoyed having me.

At the school, I was also fitting in nicely. I was assigned two biology classes in the morning and two physical education classes in the afternoon. It was no surprise that I enjoyed the PE classes a bit more than the biology classes, but both went well, most of the time.

I was young and, admittedly, somewhat anxious about teaching for the first time. I think that some of the students, especially the young ladies, could sense that. During the unit on human repro-duction in biology, some of the girls would raise their hands and ask me embarrassingly personal questions about the topic, likely just to see if I would be nervous. For the most part, however, I got along very well with the kids and I enjoyed my student teaching.

They say that we often learn best by teaching, and I found that especially true in my case. Not only did I learn a lot about class-room management and how to make academic material interesting to kids, but I also got invaluable experience outside the classroom. Working with Tom Silva, I learned how to deal with student prob-lems—and in the athletic department, I saw firsthand how teachers and coaches could help their charges balance busy lives with lots of obligations.

By the time my assignment was up, it was nearly time for gradu-ation. I returned to Corvallis and prepared to end my college career. My graduation party would be small—just me and my mother—but that didn't bother me. I felt an incredible swell of pride when I thought back on the last four years and all that I had accomplished.

Of course, there were bittersweet elements as well. I had to say goodbye to Oregon State, Corvallis, and, especially, to Heckart Lodge and the friends that I had made there. As pleased as I was to have completed my bachelor's degree, I also felt a little pang of sadness that I was the only one of my siblings to do so.

We were all still young, that was true. They certainly could have chosen the path of higher education, but I already knew from experience that their minds were set and nothing I said was going to change them. College felt transformative for me. I felt as though I'd been washed clean and emerged as a different version of myself. I wanted my brothers and sister to have that same feeling, but I knew that I couldn't force them to do anything.

By the time my mother and I had put everything in my car and headed back to Los Angeles, I was at peace with the end of college. I was surprised when, as we were leaving Corvallis, my mother turned to me and said: "You know, I'm really going to miss coming up here for Mother's Day. Coming up here made me feel really good. Important."

I knew my mother had enjoyed the yearly celebrations, but I hadn't realized before that conversation just how much they meant to her. My mother did not have an easy life, raising five children more or less on her own. She had struggled and sacrificed to keep us all fed and clothed, with a roof over our heads, and she was still able to find the time to nurture our interests and passions. During that long drive home, I mused a lot on that idea. My mother was important—incredibly important—and I could never have done all the things I was so proud of without her care and advice. I vowed that those Mother's Day celebrations weren't going to be the last time that my mother felt honored for the incredible job she had done raising us all.

If graduating felt like one kind of entrance to adulthood, this conversation and the ideas it brought up felt like another. I had armed myself with knowledge and experience, and now I had also looked at my own past and recognized all the things that had allowed me to succeed. I felt ready for the working world.

CHAPTER SIX

"We're Not Ready for an African-American Coach"

I f my knee injury had taught me nothing else, it had taught me the importance of always having a backup plan. After I graduated from Oregon State, I knew that I wanted to pursue both teaching and coaching, but I also knew that I needed a job that was readily available.

The previous fall, while I was home on Thanksgiving vacation, I had met up with a few of my friends who were senior employees with the Los Angeles County Parks and Recreation Department. They had persuaded me to take a test that would determine my fitness to join that department. It would be something to fall back on, they suggested, if I needed a job after graduation.

Since that wound up being just the case, I called them up shortly after I got back home and inquired about the job. They still had an opening, and I had done well on the test—so, in short order, I joined the Parks Department. I was especially determined to get a steady job, because this was also about the time that I proposed to my long-time girlfriend, June. I wanted to be sure that I could support her and any children we might decide to have.

I stayed at the Parks Department for a year, but I never forgot my real ambition: coaching. I discovered that, even after graduating from Oregon State, I still needed to take a few more teaching courses before I qualified for a teacher's credential in California. I enrolled in a number of courses that year while I worked for the county parks. Soon, I had made up the credits and achieved certification.

Once I became a certified teacher, I started working as a substitute in area schools. I found myself returning to Compton Union High School District in various capacities. It wasn't long before I was offered a position as a physical education teacher at Enterprise Junior High School. In the early 1960s, Compton was very different than the city it is today. At that time, it was predominantly White and very suburban. Already, though, things were changing, as anti-discrimination laws had finally made it illegal to openly bar Black families from buying houses in certain neighborhoods. Compton bordered on historically Black Watts, and many middle-class, African-American families were slowly making their way into the more affluent Compton.

When I arrived at Compton for my first teaching job, I was still very much a novelty. For example, whenever the vice principal of the school needed to address a disciplinary problem, he would call me into his office as a kind of "backup." I was okay with this extra responsibility at first but, as time went on, it began to get pretty annoying. Every time I was called away from class, I had to go find someone to cover for me; then, upon my return, I had to catch up with whatever I had missed. I never brought this to the attention of the vice principal, however, because he was generally a nice and well-meaning man. There was nothing malicious in his request to have me on hand for disciplinary situations. I had learned a long time ago how to pick my battles.

For the most part, though, Enterprise Junior High School was a positive environment. I was particularly excited to work with the football team. Even though they were a junior high school, they were in a very competitive league with several other junior high schools in the area. It was an ideal situation for me, and they were offering a competitive salary of $5,600 per year. At that time, that was fine for a teacher just starting out.

At the same time, I was also in contact with some of my friends from Oregon State who had signed with national football teams. They were signing contracts for anywhere from $10,000 to $12,000 per year, which offers a stark picture of the differences between today's financial climate for athletes and the systems of the past. However, there were a few superstars who were earning upwards of $20,000 or $30,000 dollars, plus incentives and bonuses.

Though my salary was comparatively modest, my family and I were living well, and it seemed to me that I would continue on this path, eventually becoming a high school football coach, a position that would offer a salary increase. At this same time, my wife told me that we would soon be having a child. Naturally, we were incredibly excited. When we found out that we would be having a boy, we decided we wanted to name him "Earnel Durden." We didn't, however, want to saddle a child with a "junior" designation, so we decided to add "Michael" to the front of his name. As it turned out, he would always be called Michael and never Earnel.

Michael was the apple of my eye, and wherever I went, he went with me. From the park where I went to practice my basketball shooting to the long rides in the car, I took him along. He delighted me from the very beginning of his life. I was so happy to have a son.

By the age of three, Michael was already taller than most toddlers his age. He was growing so quickly that my wife and I couldn't help but speculate about what he might look like as an adult; we imagined that he would probably be a very tall man. We asked his pediatrician at one of his regular checkups and if he could make any predictions about Michael's future height. The doctor indicated that, in his opinion, Michael would likely be taller than average.

It may have been a little bit early to be thinking about such things, but I was very excited about this news. I hoped that, if I had a tall, strong son, he would be more inclined toward athletics. I was really looking forward to sharing my passions with my child.

Michael's birth had only encouraged me to continue to move forward with my career. While I enjoyed my job at Enterprise, I knew that I wanted to move beyond coaching junior high. At that time, it was customary to only pay teachers ten months out of the year. June and I divided my total salary into twelve months, so that we could budget properly for the entire year. This method also gave me the opportunity to go back to school during the summer months without having to worry about picking up a second job to cover the bills for those additional two months. I was eager to get more education. Not only would it make me a more desirable employee in the future, but in the Compton school system, each class I completed came with a bump in pay.

So back to school I went, still carrying a full load of teaching responsibilities and coaching after school. My classroom day ended at 3 o'clock, my coaching day ended at 6 p.m., and by 7:30 p.m., I found myself back in the classroom—his time as a student at one of the area universities. It was difficult to balance all of my obligations, but taking all the available support classes was one way that I could increase my salary at Compton as well as make myself a more attractive candidate for future positions.

It wasn't long before I was able to move on from the junior high level. I put in a request to teach at Compton High School and they offered me a job teaching PE. I was the first African-American physical education teacher at Compton High. These days, when I tell people that part of my history, they don't believe me. Compton has become so synonymous with African Americans in Los Angeles that it's difficult to remember that, not so long ago, Compton was a fervently White city.

Along with the PE class, I was also given World Cultures and Biology classes to teach—but when I took the job, the understanding was that I would become the full-time PE teacher and possibly the next head football coach. At that time in my career, I couldn't imagine a better position.

At Compton High School, I was also asked to develop a wrestling program. The request wasn't quite as out-of-left-field as it seemed. I did have a bit of experience with collegiate wrestling because, during my senior year at Oregon State, when I was nursing my knee injury, I had spent time with the wrestling team and I'd picked up a lot of information. With this in mind, I set to work creating a high school wrestling program.

It turned out to be a real challenge. During my first year as wrestling coach, we were only able to get nine people to go out for wrestling—nine students out of a student body of 2,700. It seemed that students in California just weren't as aware of collegiate wrestling as the students in Oregon were. For my students, their main—or only—exposure to wrestling came from what they saw on television.

It was a chore to get kids excited about this sport, because most of them had, at best, a very skewed understanding. In the beginning, it was tough to build up a critical mass and get things up and running.

Over time, however, the program did start to fall into place. During my second year as coach, we were able to get a full contingent of prospects and, during my third year, we sent eleven of our thirteen team members to the CIF (California Interscholastic Federation) championships. This turnaround really impressed local coaches in the area. More than once, we had colleagues from other schools coming around to ask exactly how we had done it.

Though I was succeeding at Compton High and enjoying my time there, I found that, once again, I had developed a case of itchy feet. I knew that I was ready to coach at the collegiate level, and I wanted to expand my horizons wherever possible. In those days, Compton Community College was known simply as Compton JC. It was also widely known as a powerhouse football factory and was well-regarded for its athletic prowess.

At the time, there were playoffs each year between all the JCs in the Los Angeles area, and these games determined which teams would compete in the "Junior Rose Bowl." Just as the name implied, the Junior Rose Bowl (also called the Pasadena Bowl) was to Junior College football what the Rose Bowl was to Big Ten and PAC Twelve football.

Every year, Compton JC seemed to come out on top of this competition. Usually, they ended up facing the top junior college team, which was out of Tyler, Texas. Nearly every year, the Texans would come to Pasadena and really put on a show with their student body. Compton students had no trouble, however, rising to the occasion and bringing an incredible display of their own.

Compton had some amazing athletes at the time, some of whom were veterans attending on the GI Bill and planning to eventually transfer to a four-year college. Others simply wanted to be part of a great program. Athletes like Joe "The Jet" Perry and Hugh McElhenny—who went on to play for the San Francisco 49ers—spent time at Compton JC before going on to become pro football players.

These days, Compton Community College no longer exists—it has been absorbed by El Camino College as a satellite campus and it sits, unassuming and nearly unregarded, along the 91 freeway. To drive by it, a person would never guess that the modest buildings were once the site of athletic high achievement and football glory.

When I was starting out in my teaching career, however,

Compton JC was an obvious choice for anyone who wanted ex-perience with collegiate football. I applied to the college and, sure enough, I was accepted there for a position as a teacher and assis-tant football coach. On Tuesdays and Thursdays, I taught a class on communicable diseases. That left Mondays, Wednesdays, and Fridays free for meetings with any students who wanted to discuss their assignments.

I served as assistant coach under Coach Ramsey, who was a very nice guy and a fine coach. I really appreciated working with some-one so personable and so knowledgeable. With Coach Ramsey at the helm, we had an excellent win-loss record at Compton Junior College.

Soon, I was contacted by Long Beach State University. They were interested in hiring me to be part of their football staff on the strength of our record. They had also apparently heard about the wrestling program that I had put together at Compton High School, and they offered me a position as Head Wrestling Coach as well. I turned down the wrestling job, feeling that I didn't really have enough familiarity with the sport, but I did take the job as assistant football coach and PE teacher, with the understanding that I would join the staff the following semester.

I was still working with Compton JC and Coach Ramsey when I first heard about Tommy Prothro putting on a clinic. By this time, Coach Prothro had moved from Oregon State back to UCLA—this time as the head football coach. He would be hosting this clinic at the Shrine Auditorium near USC. Both Coach Ramsey and I were eager to attend.

The seminar was interesting and, afterwards, I hung back to say hello to Coach Prothro. We exchanged some small talk and, as I turned to go, he called me back.

"Earnel," he said, "do you have a little time?"

"Yeah," I answered.

"Could we have a cup of coffee together?"

Of course I said yes, and we went around the corner to a small coffee stand where Coach Prothro wasted no time getting to the point. He wanted to offer me a job working with him at UCLA. I definitely had not been expecting this, but I couldn't deny that it was an attractive idea. I couldn't imagine many coaches I'd rather work with. The Bruins were a great team and UCLA was a great university.

My choice was complicated, however, by the fact that I had actually just committed to coaching and teaching PE at Long Beach State University. When I'd accepted the job, it had seemed like a great opportunity—and it was. But now I felt like my commitment to Long Beach was preventing me from pursuing a really remarkable position with the Bruins.

I told Coach Prothro that I had agreed to teach at Long Beach but that I was reasonably sure I could discharge my obligation to them after the first semester and come over to UCLA at the winter break. Of course, I did not tell anyone at Long Beach about Coach Prothro's offer or my intentions to leave. As it turned out, it was a very good thing that I had lined up another opportunity, because Long Beach State was probably the worst job I ever had.

The school was located right on the border of the overwhelmingly White Orange County and, in those days, the atmosphere was very unfriendly for African Americans. I learned that firsthand when the head of my department organized a get-acquainted dinner at his home. At one point, June and I found ourselves chatting with the department head's mother, an older White woman who was, at least initially, polite.

The conversation took a hard turn when she said to my wife, in a tone of disbelief, "I hope you folks aren't planning on moving into this area?"

She was clearly horrified by the idea that a young Black family might live anywhere near "her" neighborhood, and she had no qualms about expressing that to our shocked faces. My department head overheard this exchange and hurried over to admonish her for talking to us like that. Her sentiments, however, were hardly unique. Few other people were so direct with their views, but they made their feelings plain in other ways.

When I first arrived at Long Beach, the coaching staff had been welcoming. As time wore on, however, they seemed increasingly distant. It was difficult for me to make friends or even have positive working relationships with some of my colleagues.

I was given the responsibility of coaching the defensive backs and I served as head coach for the freshman team. I wasted no time in hiring some student assistants to help with the freshmen, because most of my time was devoted to the varsity team.

Even though I spent the bulk of my time working with the varsity players, I was never invited to any of the varsity games. Somehow, during our scheduled games, I always wound up being sent on tours to scout the next team we would play. This was fine with me until I learned that no one was even bothering to look at or read what I'd written about those very teams I was supposed to be evaluating. It became increasingly clear that these trips were just a way of keeping me far away from the games.

Ironically, even as I was being kept away from the varsity games, my freshman team was thriving. They were undefeated that season and their performance was a stark contrast to the varsity team, which was struggling. The varsity coaching staff seemed frustrated with how their season was going. I had even heard that some of the varsity coaches openly were saying they hoped our freshman team would lose upcoming games, presumably so the varsity team would look better in comparison, though perhaps it was simple spite. I don't know if this rumor was true, but the coaches on my freshman staff were genuinely upset when they passed this information on to me.

After such a string of good experiences with teaching and coaching, it was difficult to be thrust into this strange atmosphere where my coworkers seemed to be actively undermining me. Even aside from the daily emotional and spiritual toll that it took on me, I was being shut out of many elements of coaching. I was not getting the important experience that I needed from the position. With all of my jobs, I strove to become a better teacher. As I had during my other jobs, I was also continuing my education at Long Beach State, working toward a master's degree. Working all day teaching and coaching really put a strain on my preparation for my next degree, which was a significant challenge in its own right.

My master's committee was demanding, and each and every one of my experiments had to meet with their approval. They insisted that every element of my research be perfect. Once I finally finished my classes and had gotten my research approved by the committee, the last step was getting the material professionally typed and submitted to the library for their approval. After months of hard work, the library finally accepted my thesis, and a ton of pressure was lifted from my shoulders.

The athletic director at that time was a good friend of mine named Fred Miller. He had a son about Michael's age and the two boys spent a lot of time together at sleepovers and play dates. Fred was also the head of my master's program, which was made up of five individuals there at LB state. I was so happy to have a friend in a position of authority in my program, especially when it seemed that so many other people in the academic hierarchy were either ambivalent or hostile toward me.

Fred was one of the first people I told about my offer from UCLA and my plans to accept. He tried to talk me out of it and convince me to stay at Long Beach, but despite being the Athletic

Director, he didn't really have an understanding of what was going on in the department—at least, not when it came to my treatment. I liked Fred, but not enough to stay in a toxic environment where my growth as a teacher and coach was being stymied.

I also had to consider my responsibilities to my family. The position with UCLA would be higher profile and would allow me more room to develop as a coach. My career was more important than ever now. Just before I started at Long Beach State, June had told me that our second child was on the way. Michael was three-and-a-half years old, and we were hoping that we would have a little girl, for a matching set. Instead, Michael got a little brother named Kevin. Within another year and a half, he got another brother. We never did have that girl.

A daughter would have been wonderful, but I couldn't have been happier with my boys. As someone who loved athletics—so much so that I had made it my life's work—I had always hoped my kids would be similarly interested in sports. With three boys, I figured I had three good chances at a child who shared my passions. During this time, I had also begun to dabble in real estate. June and I purchased a two-bedroom duplex in Inglewood for $24,000 with 10 percent down. The house was more than just a starter home, however. We decided to live in one of the units and rent out the other side. Thus, our adventures in real estate began.

After the semester break, my little family and I moved into Inglewood and I went to UCLA to be an assistant coach. Once again, I found myself the first African American in a given position, this time on UCLA's coaching staff—I was the first African-American football coach in the school's history. The local newspapers really latched on to this story, interviewing both Coach Prothro and me, and it was big news in LA for a while.

UCLA football coaches staff – kneeling, from left, are assistant coaches Jerry Long, Tony Kopay, John Becker (head frosh coach), Bobb McKittrick and Fred Von Appen. Standing, from left, are assistant coaches Earnel Durden, Larrye Weaver, head coach Tommy Prothro, and assistants Dick Vermeil and Rich Brooks.

While Los Angeles was more diverse than Orange County and UCLA was a much larger school, I would still have my share of difficult situations dealing with people who were uncomfortable with a Black coworker—or perhaps they were just uncomfortable with me. The difference, however, was in how those situations were handled by the athletic department, especially by Coach Prothro himself.

Early on in my career at UCLA, I was told about the high value placed on recruitment. If we had a recruit on campus, we were to pay as much attention to them as possible. I took this advice to heart as I started going out to local high schools to examine the athletes.

At Gardena High School, I began recruiting a nice young man who played guard. He was a good-sized boy and a fine football player, and I thought he would make a great addition to the team. I invited him to attend one of our practices and, after the practice was over, I spoke to him privately and told him a bit more about what we were doing with the team and what he, as a player, could expect.

After I had dismissed the recruit, I met up with the other coaches. It was immediately clear that the offensive coordinator did not like how I had managed my time. He thought it was wrong for me to have spent time talking to the recruit instead of debriefing with the team.

I pointed out what I had been told about the importance of the recruits and how I was supposed to spend as much time with them as possible. The recruits, I reminded him, were supposed to be our first priority. He didn't particularly appreciate my response, and soon we were arguing over the issue. Eventually, Coach Prothro came in and we shelved the argument.

At the end of that year, Coach Prothro dismissed the offensive coordinator, and I couldn't help but wonder if it had been because of our argument. I finally asked Coach Prothro: "Did you fire the offensive coordinator because of me?"

Coach Prothro was very honest with me. "Yes," he said. "It was at least partially because of you."

I wasn't sure what that meant. Had it been my disagreement with the coordinator, or the general attitude he seemed to have toward me and his job, or his approach to the game? I never found out specifically what his reasoning was, but I took that interaction with Coach Prothro to heart. It was clear to me then that this job was going to be fundamentally different from Long Beach, where none of the people working above me really seemed to notice or care about shoddy treatment that was directed at me, often because of my race. Coach Prothro had made it clear to me that I was a valued part of his team once again.

I was quickly learning that, just as Coach Prothro was an idiosyncratic football coach who had a low-key approach to dealing with the players on his team, he also had his own ways of dealing with his staff. For example, he had an interesting method of testing his new assistant coaches. He would invite them to a game of chess. I had heard a bit about this practice of his, so I wasn't surprised when, one day, he invited me into his office and asked me if I played chess.

"A little," I said. I had actually played the occasional game in my spare time, but I knew that I was much less experienced than Coach Prothro. He was notoriously good at bridge and he was also a very accomplished chess player, so I was a bit surprised when our first game was quite close.

Coach asked to play a second game and, that time, it was not close at all and he beat me far and away. I'm not sure what my performance told him about me as an assistant coach, but it seemed that this ritual offered him some sort of information. At the very least, the chess games seemed to set a tone for the relationship between Coach Prothro and the men working with him.

Those years at UCLA were some of the happiest of my life. As it had been in so many other places, I stood out as an African-American man in a White atmosphere. Slowly but surely, however, people began to accept and even embrace me. It was during this time in my life that I made some of my most enduring friendships.

I was first introduced to Dick Vermeil during these years. He had come in to take over the newly vacant offensive coordinator position, and we hit it off right away. I liked Dick's approach to the game and I also liked that he was a positive thinker when it came to football. I quickly recognized his clever way of attacking the defenses. I stuck close to him because I wanted to learn as much from him as possible.

Most of that first year—after I joined UCLA, in the winter of 1968—was a process of soaking up as much information as I could from the people around me. I wanted to learn everything there was to know about the game, my fellow coaches, and— perhaps most importantly—the athletes. I had been hired as a running back coach, so I concentrated my energy on the athletes who would be our running backs. I wanted to have a good working knowledge of their strengths and their weaknesses so I could say, at a moment's notice, who we could use in a certain situation and who was better suited to other plays.

We had several running backs who could do a great job, but Mickey Cureton and Greg Jones were our two featured backs. Both were incredible players and key parts of our 1970 team. The 1970 team was by far our best. We were undefeated that year, until the fateful game with Stanford at Palo Alto.

The game had actually been going well and it looked like we were going to have an easy win when our featured back, Mickey Cureton, went up the middle on a dive play and took a bad fall, injuring his neck.

Naturally, we had the team doctor examine Mickey immediately, and the news was not good: Mickey had broken his neck. This was one of the worst possible outcomes for everyone involved. We continued the game, eventually tying Stanford, but I knew that everyone's mind was on Mickey and his uncertain future.

Our whole team was in shock on the way home and our hearts were heavy as we contemplated what was in store for Mickey. He was only a junior and, before that game, everyone had assumed he had a long career ahead of him. Now, we were all asking ourselves if he would ever be able to play again.

Mickey was an all-purpose back and he had the speed and agility that the position demanded. Like all great backs, he had that ability to make people miss. He showed so much promise, which made his injury all the more tragic. I couldn't help but think about my own history.

I knew what it felt like to seemingly be poised for great success and then find it all vanished in a moment, because of a freak accident. I had been where Mickey was, though his injury was more severe than mine. I knew the fear and anxiety and pain he must be feeling.

It was too soon, however, to say exactly what was going to happen. We still didn't know the extent of Mickey's injury and, though it certainly sounded bad, players have come back from similar accidents. We were all hoping that he would be able to play again—maybe not that season or the next, but someday.

As it turned out, our hopes would be dashed. Mickey's neck injury simply presented too great a risk for any doctor to declare him fit. If he went out onto the field and injured his neck again, he might suffer even more serious effects, and no medical professional was going to let him take that chance.

It was a terrible situation but, just as my college team had continued in my absence, UCLA could not stop because of any one player. After the Stanford game, we had an upcoming game against our crosstown rivals, USC. At that point in the season, we were undefeated.

Of course, when we played each other, it didn't really matter what the record was. Most of the game went well for us. We were in the lead with only a minute left in play when USC's quarterback Jimmy Jones threw a pass to Sam Dickerson, deep in the end zone. That pass took them all the way to the Rose Bowl that year. Naturally, this was a heartbreaker for our team and the coaching staff.

We'd had the Rose Bowl in our grasp and had watched it slip away. Needless to say, there was considerable unhappiness after our defeat.

Shortly thereafter, we started getting reports that players were taking the loss hard. The coaches approached players to help wherever they could. I knew, though, that no coach, no matter how well intentioned, could soothe this pain. Only time would help now.

Sure enough, as the weeks and months went on, we managed to put the last season behind us. All of us—especially the coaching staff— were trying to look forward as we embarked upon a serious new recruiting campaign. Every coach was assigned an area that he was to cover.

One day, Coach Prothro called me into his office and told me that one of his coaches was preparing to retire. He wanted me to take over the man's recruiting responsibilities in Texas. I made arrangements through our team secretary for flights and hotel accommodations in Dallas, and the first thing I did upon my arrival was make contact with our departing coach. He, in turn, introduced me to some UCLA alumni, who were helpful in the recruiting process. He also introduced me to some of the staff of the Dallas Cowboys, who went out of their way to accommodate me in every way—they even set up a room where I could watch films of the local high school athletes.

Dallas became my home base as I headed out to various smaller cities and towns in Texas. The Dallas Cowboys made a list each year of all the good high school athletes in the state of Texas, the ones that they thought might become excellent football players. I, naturally, was interested in some of these players as well, and I traveled all over the state meeting with them.

One evening, when the coach and I were having dinner, he said something that sounded strange to me. "Earnel," he said, "I find that African Americans in the South are very different from African Americans in the North."

This statement caught me by surprise. I looked up and asked, "What's the difference?"

He simply smiled and said, "You'll find out."

I never really got a straight answer about what he'd meant, but I did notice certain things as I continued to work with young athletes. I found that, in general, the mothers were key figures in African-American families in the South. The fathers of the boys I recruited tended to be somewhat passive, while the mothers were more significant forces in the lives of their children. Texas mothers also were active in their churches and they were, seemingly universally, interested in knowing the recruiter's philosophy along those lines.

Those were the major differences that I noticed during my time as recruiter, but I have heard that White people see things very differently than Black people when race is involved.

Eventually I, along with the other coaches, returned to UCLA campus in anticipation of the new season. The coaching staff had scattered, each of us going into our designated area to seek out the best possible athletes. When we reconvened and saw, for the first time, all of the new recruits, it was clear almost immediately that we had brought together one of the best recruiting classes in UCLA history.

Still, I was surprised—and so was Dick Vermeil—when, after the recruiting season was over, Coach Prothro called us into his office to congratulate us on a fine year. He was not a man given to excessive praise—he always figured that we were being paid to do a good job, so unless we had done something truly outstanding, we did not expect a pat on the back. We knew from his atypical reaction that he was especially pleased with the athletes we had recruited that year. It truly was an incredible crop of young men.

I don't remember the names of all of my recruits from that season, but I know that a few of those gentlemen went on to play in the National Football League. They were some of the greatest high school football players in the area. We had out-recruited the PAC 10 teams as well as some of the teams outside of our conference. We all felt that these young men would keep our team amongst the elite in the country as we headed into another season.

While I was working at UCLA, I had not abandoned my fledgling real estate endeavors. June and I had gone in with another couple on a three-bedroom house in California City. It was a nice town, located about ten miles north of the Palmdale/Lancaster area in the Mojave Desert. We would take turns with the other family going up to what we called "the cabin" on weekends.

One weekend, June had asked me to fetch something from the store, so I headed out to get it. The cabin was far enough from Los Angeles that it felt like an escape to go out there, but I still wanted to stay connected, even just over the weekend. So I picked up a copy of the *Los Angeles Times* while I was at the store.

Of course, I immediately flipped to the sports section. I was shocked when I read the headline: Tommy Prothro Takes the Job With the LA Rams for $100,000!

$100,000 was a lot of money in 1970, and Coach Prothro was a big name in college football, so of course this was news. What surprised me, however, was the fact that I hadn't heard a single thing about it before that day. I'd had no idea that Coach Prothro was even considering a different position, let alone in negotiations with a professional team.

I called Coach Prothro right away to get the story from the horse's mouth. He confirmed that he was indeed heading to the Rams and, what's more, he wanted to take me along with him. For a moment, I was speechless. After gathering myself, I stammered out a, "Yes, of course." The chance to work on a professional team was almost too good to be true, especially for someone relatively early in my career, as I was.

Upon returning to UCLA, I was informed that only five of the nine coaches had received invitations to go on with Coach Prothro to the Rams. For me, the situation was bittersweet. I had really enjoyed working at UCLA. I liked the people, I liked the environment, and I had no idea what was waiting for us with the Rams. I'd had little experience with professional football teams.

The Rams had been having some public problems recently. Their owner was dying, and he apparently didn't want the existing coach to stay on after his death. He had given Coach Prothro almost everything he wanted to entice him into the job for this reason. I imagined that, on a professional team, the politicking and interpersonal conflict must be exponentially greater than it was in college sports, and that was a little bit worrisome.

I was happy, however, that some of the coaches who had been with me at UCLA would also be coming along to the Rams. I knew that this was an incredible opportunity for me. At the same time, I knew that would never forget my time at UCLA, which had offered me so much.

During the fall of 1971, we began our coaching responsibilities with the Los Angeles Rams—with a small amount of trepidation and a great deal of excitement.

CHAPTER SEVEN

On the Rams with Coach Prothro

As I prepared to start with the Rams, I couldn't help but reflect upon how surreal my current situation was. Though I had spent much of my adolescence dreaming of playing in the National Football League, it had never even occurred to me that I might coach an NFL team—let alone the Los Angeles Rams, who had loomed so large in my own childhood.

When I was a kid, the LA Rams had seemed truly larger than life. A few friends and I would head for the Coliseum and find a way into a game, every chance we got. I loved watching stars like Bob Waterfield, Paul "Tank" Younger, "Deacon" Dan Towler, Elroy "Crazy Legs" Hirsch, and Tom Fears, just to name a few. These players were my heroes. I never imagined that I would be in any way connected with them.

Of course, by the time that I was working with the Rams, most of the players that I remembered from my boyhood had long since retired. Nevertheless, I still felt the weight of the Rams legacy as I prepared to take up my new position. At the same time, I was also part of another kind of legacy: once again, I was the first African-American coach in Rams history. Once again, the newspapers picked up the story and ran with it, and I felt the familiar pressure

of being the first to a position and knowing there would be special expectations that went along with it. The *Los Angeles Times* and
other news media made a big deal about my hiring, so I was always
aware that there were many eyes upon me.

TOGETHER AGAIN—L.A. Rams' newly appointed head
football coach Tommy Prothro brought his trusted assistant, Earnel Durden, along with him from UCLA. Durden won All-American honors for Prothro as a wingback
at Oregon State. Prothro made Durden the first black
assistant coach in Ram history.

Prothro Did It

This column conductor has been pleading, praying
and begging the Los Angeles Rams to integrate their
coaching staff for years, long before it became fash-
ionable to hire blacks as coaches. Before the ink was
dry on his contract, Tom-
my Prothro had his ex-
UCLA assistant, Earnel
Durden, in the Rams fold
as the club's first black
assistant in history.

Prothro made
Durden the first
black assistant foot-
ball coach in the his-
tory of UCLA, too.
Durden won All-City
honors and led the
town in scoring as a
prep star for Jim
Blewett at Manual
Arts High.

He went on to
gain All-American
honors as a wingback
for Prothro at Ore-
gon State. As an Ore-
gon Stater, Durden
also performed in the Rose Bowl for Prothro.

For a little man of 5-11 and only 170 pounds,
Durden was one of the most effective runners and
guttiest performers Prothro ever coached.

I asked Coach Durden, "How is it to work for
Prothro?"

"I like working for him because he puts you on
your own. The only thing he is concerned about is if
you get the job done or not.

"As a result of getting to the point where you get
the job done, in between that point you are going to
reach a period of trial and error, at which time it's
going to be a tremendous learning situation for you.

"You are completely on your own until you are
ready to present the team with whatever conclusion
you have reached. And it is at that time when he either
rejects them or accepts them.

"And you don't want too many rejections. If an
author gets too many rejections he is forced to stop
eating."

Durden didn't say the same prevails for Prothro's
assistants, but the record will show that wherever
Prothro has coached he has been successful.

Will the change from college coaching to the pros
be very difficult? Durden answered:

"I have only been here a short time, but what I
have seen so far football is football. In the pros you
have a little more talent to work with and a lot of
different types of situations you must try to solve."

On the personal side, Durden is married to the
former June Pecot of New Orleans. They have three
sons—Michael, 11; Kevin, 8, and Allan, 7.

Michael the past season tried his hand at football
as a member of the Inglewood Apaches in the All-
American League.

★   ★   ★

but UCLA

Article covering me as I joined Coach Prothro in coaching the Rams

Even as this was happening, my life was changing rapidly in other ways. With three young children in the house, it seemed that every day brought with it some new discovery or adventure. Michael, our oldest, was growing like a beanpole; sure enough, he was as tall as we had expected and handsome as well. My second son, Kevin, was turning out to be a husky fellow, just like me. Also like me, he was drawn to athletics from an early age. Our youngest son, Allan, was still really just a toddler, but he followed his brothers everywhere they went, eager to do anything they were doing. Like his older brothers, Allan became more and more interested in sports. Before we knew it, he was playing Pop Warner flag football. It was incredibly satisfying as a father to watch my boys learn to play the game that I loved.

Around the time I started with the Rams, we moved once again, purchasing a house in Del Amo Woods, just north of San Pedro and east of Palos Verdes. The house—which was in a new planned community—was beautiful, with five bedrooms and three levels. We needed the extra space with three rambunctious kids in the house.

All of the kids were very active, playing Little League baseball as well as football. Nevertheless, they still managed to get into mischief occasionally. One day, shortly before we moved out of our duplex on Manhattan Place in Inglewood, June was busy preparing for the move when she suddenly realized that she could no longer hear the distant sounds of Allan playing in his room.

She found his room empty. As she was frantically searching the rest of the house, the phone rang. It was the principal of the elementary school that both Michael and Kevin attended, which was only about a block from our home. The principal said that Allan was sitting in his office. Apparently, he had decided that he was going to visit his brothers at school!

Though our new life was exciting, there was still a part of me that was sad to leave UCLA behind. I was particularly disappointed that I would never get the opportunity to coach the young men that we had spent so much time recruiting for the Bruins. During those years at UCLA, I had put together a great recruiting team headed by Brad Pye Jr. Pye was the sports director at the time for the *Los Angeles Sentinel*, a Black-owned newspaper. We had started something great together, and it was hard for me to leave without seeing how the team eventually came together.

For me, UCLA had been a perfect place to work. I liked the environment and the people, and I liked the college atmosphere. I was so glad that I'd been able to spend the time I did there. UCLA had not been my only option for coaching at the college level, either. Around the same time that Coach Prothro offered me the job with the Bruins, I was also offered the same position at Stanford University.

I had gone up to San Francisco to meet with Coach Taylor and the team's athletic director, to discuss the job and the potential benefits of coming to Stanford. One part of their offer stood out to me in particular: As a coach at Stanford, my children would all have been eligible to attend the university for free when they came of age. It was a tempting offer, and I thought long and hard before making my decision. A few things finally tipped the scales towards UCLA, including the fact that I would not have to move my family—and, of course, I could not pass up the opportunity to work with Tommy Prothro.

In the following years, Stanford went on to participate in three Rose Bowls, led by Jim Plunkett and Randy Vataha. Despite that, I rarely found myself thinking about what it might have been like if I had taken the position at Stanford, mainly because I enjoyed my time at UCLA so much. Now I found myself once again facing a difficult career crossroads. I could only hope that coaching for the Rams would be as rewarding as UCLA had been.

Before we even got started, however, there was rampant speculation about why Coach Prothro had left UCLA to take the job with the Rams. The newspapers reported all sorts of theories, some true and some wholly imagined. I didn't pay much attention to this because I already knew who Tommy Prothro was, and he was not the sort of man to do anything without thinking it through carefully first.

We were hired in the spring of 1970. The time gap before the season began gave our staff the chance to bring in our new players for a getting-acquainted session. The players were both curious and cautious. We, as coaches, were definitely eager to get to know our players and see how they would fit into our scheme of things.

It was clear right away that the players were trying their best to size us up. As far as they were concerned, we were a bunch of college coaches coming in to tell them how to win NFL games. Mostly, they seemed interested in what we had to say and curious about how our strategy would differ from that of previous coaches. A few individuals, however, were skeptical about some of our techniques, and they let us know how they felt. I suspected that those particular players would have been disagreeable no matter who the new coaches were.

Organized practices began in March of 1970 and lasted until June of that year. We always took the month of June off. The rookies reported to training camp around the middle of July. Our schedule had to be slightly compressed, however, because the Rams were scheduled to play in the Hall of Fame game in Canton, Ohio, which was the first game of the year.

Everyone had to hit the ground running. The learning curve was steep for all of us, but I felt that I was learning in some unexpected ways. In 1970, there were only three other African-American coaches in the National Football League. One was Emlen Tunnel of the New York Giants. Tunnell, who coached the defensive backs for the Giants, had also been the first Black player on the New York Giants and the first Black player inducted into the Pro-Football Hall of Fame in Canton, Ohio.

The Cleveland Browns had Al Tabor, who had played quarterback for Tuskegee Institute in Tuskegee, Alabama before becoming the first Black player signed to professional football in 1949. Last—but certainly not least—there was Lionel Taylor, who coached the receivers on the Pittsburgh Steelers. He'd also had a storied playing career of his own as a wide receiver for the Bears, the Broncos, and the Oilers. Even though the number of African-American coaches in the NFL was (very slowly) growing, I knew the sport was far from fully integrated.

I was surprised to find out that nearly all the NFL teams put quotas on the number of Black players that they were willing to put on their teams. This was not set down in any rulebooks, but was simply unspoken knowledge, a practice that a lot of coaches engaged in. By the time I started with the Rams, however, this was already becoming less and less common. It was not social evolution or racial enlightenment that had made the change, but rather the enormous pressure to win that the coaches faced. Coaches would rather draft the best players available than obey the arbitrary guidelines about the racial makeup of the team.

While the teams soon found themselves with more and more Black players, there were still many limits on what an African American could do in professional football. Many of these limitations were fueled by strange and baseless myths about the capabilities of Black players. It may seem incredible now, but in those days, it was widely believed that Black players simply couldn't handle certain positions. The center position, for example, was thought to be too much for African-American players, mainly because it required the center to call out defensive fronts and blocking techniques. Many White coaches believed that African-American players weren't smart enough to juggle all of these things during a fast-paced game.

For similar reasons, Black players were often kept out of the middle linebacker position. The middle linebacker is a key player in the defensive scheme who needs to recognize the offensive front and put the defense into position to attack. They coordinate with the defensive backs so that they can call the correct coverage. The middle linebacker is also responsible for whatever blitzes the team has conjured up for that particular game. The position was considered too challenging for a Black player. Willie Lanier, who played for the Kansas City Chiefs, was one of the first truly successful players to put the lie to this idea. He played middle linebacker for Kansas City and went on to be All-Pro for several years.

The free safety, another position that required strategic thinking, was also frequently closed to African-American players. Free safeties are responsible for calling the coverage of the defensive backs. This role is critical to the defense, because correct coverage is vital, especially against great receivers. There have been so many amazing free safeties of color since then that it's nearly impossible for me to say who has been the most outstanding. However, Kermit Alexander and Ronnie Lott are two that stand out in my mind at present.

Of course, the quarterback—perhaps the most mythologized of all football positions—was almost never offered to a Black player. It has often been said that "as the quarterback goes, so goes the game." The position is incredibly important, and a good quarterback definitely can carry a team to victory. Even if a team has every other element in place and on point, a bad quarterback can keep a good team from becoming great. These positions often allowed players to function as coaches on the field, evaluating the game and directing play as it was happening. White coaches were reluctant to put such a pivotal responsibility in the hands of Black players, whom they believed to be less reliable in challenging situations.

Nowadays, these ideas seem bizarre and unfounded. We have seen so many successful Black quarterbacks since then that it seems almost laughable that anyone would ever have really believed that one's race could actually make them unfit for a football position. One of my favorite quarterbacks, Warren Moon, actually launched his career in the Canadian Football League because no NFL team would draft him as a quarterback. It was only after he had broken all the Canadian records that the National Football League allowed him to play. He joined the Houston Oilers (now known as the Tennessee Titans), where he was an immediate and smashing success, making All-Pro almost every year. To this day, he is recognized as one of the best quarterbacks in the National Football League's history.

Each of these players who came into a position that had been previously closed to African Americans and excelled there put a little crack in the barriers that professional football placed on Black athletes. Nevertheless, it took decades and countless talented athletes performing at their peak to really banish these unspoken rules of the game. Today, over 60 percent of the players in the National Football League are Black, and we see athletes of color in every position the game has to offer.

For the most part, the public never knew why certain players never occupied certain positions, or why the racial makeup of the teams was so uniform across the league. These were hidden practices, but when I joined the Rams, I got a frontline look at exactly how the sausage was made.

In 1971, the Rams brought John Walton on board as a quarterback. John was drafted out of Elizabeth City University; he was a backup to our regular quarterback, Roman Gabriel, who had been the Rams's quarterback for the past five years.

1971 LOS ANGELES RAMS
8 Wins, 5 Losses, 1 Tie

FRONT ROW (L-R) – George Menefee, head trainer; Isiah Robertson, Kermit Alexander, Lance Rentzel, Jack Snow, Pat Curran, Bob Klein, Dean Halverson, Joe Scibelli, Jim Nettles, John Pergine, Marlin McKeever, Roger Williams, David Ray and Cash Birdwell, trainer.

THIRD ROW (L-R) – Dr. Jules Rasinski, Jr., team physician; Tommy Prothro, head coach; Alvin Haymond, Travis Williams, Rich Saul, David Jones, Jerry Rhome, Dave Elmendorf, Willie Ellison, Joe Carollo, Clarence Williams, Coy Bacon, Les Josephson, Don Hewitt, equipment manager; Sid Hall, defensive line coach; and Bobb McKittrick, offensive line coach.

SECOND ROW (L-R) – Dick Vermeil, quarterback coach; Larry Smith, Jack Reynolds, Mike LaHood, Matt Maslowski, John Walton, Lee White, Jim Purnell, Ken Geddes, Pat Studstill, Bob Thomas, Gene Howard, Rick Cash, Leon McLaughlin, offensive line coach; and Leroy Lake, Blair Field superintendent.

FOURTH ROW (L-R) – Larrye Weaver, defensive backfield coach; Tom Catlin, linebacker coach; Jack Youngblood, Phil Olsen, Bill Nelson, Tom Mack, Merlin Olsen, Ken Iman, Roman Gabriel, Riah Busin, Greg Wojnik Charlie Cowan, Harry Schuh, Rich Brooks, general assignments coach; Bow-Wow, chief of security; and Earnel Durden, offensive backfield coach.

1971 Rams Hilites Film · Reserve Now · Call 277-4700

In 1972, the Rams also picked up James Harris, on waivers from the Tampa Bay Buccaneers. Both young men were African-American.

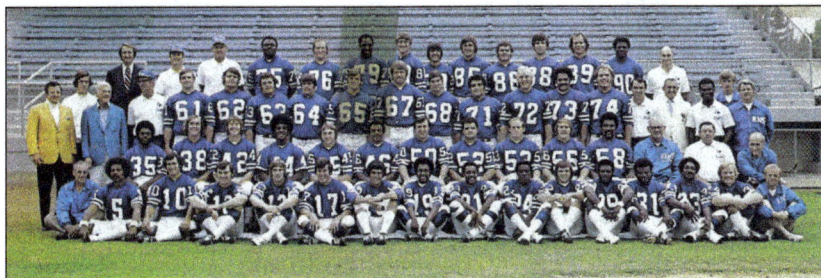

1972 LOS ANGELES RAMS

BOTTOM ROW (L-to-R): Leroy Lake, equipment asst.; Dick Gordon, Dave Chapple, Pete Beathard, Lance Rentzel, Leo Hart, Roman Gabriel, Jim Nettles, Gene Howard, Clarence Williams, David Ray, Joe Sweet, Larry McCutcheon, Willie Ellison, Les Josephson, Cash Birdwell, trainer.
SECOND ROW: Bobby Thomas, Larry Smith, Dave Elmendorf, Al Clark, Jim Bertelsen, Roger Williams, Ken Iman, John Pergine, Jim Purnell, Dean Halverson, Isiah Robertson, Tommy Prothro, head coach; Sid Hall, asst. coach; George Menefee, head trainer.
THIRD ROW: Don Klosterman, asst. to owner; Carroll Rosenbloom, owner; Leon McLaughlin, asst. coach; Rich Saul, Willie Parker, Joe Carollo, Jack Reynolds, Tom Mack, Bill Nelson, Mike LaHood, Joe Scibelli, Phil Olsen, Charles Cowan, Merlin Olsen, Rich Brooks, asst. coach; "Bow Wow", security; Earnel Durden, asst. coach; Tim Ryan, ball boy; Don Hewitt, equipment manager.
TOP ROW: Matt McCann, ball boy; Dr. Jules Rasinski, team physician; Dick Vermeil, asst. coach; Tom Catlin, asst. coach; John Williams, Harry Schuh, Coy Bacon, Bob Klein, Jack Snow, Jack Youngblood, Marlin McKeever, Pat Curran, Fred Dryer, Larry Brooks, Bobb McKittrick, asst. coach.

James Harris had been drafted by Tampa Bay in the first round but, in my opinion, Tampa had never really utilized him properly. I was curious to know exactly what had happened at Tampa, because James had come out of Grambling State University with a great reputation as an excellent quarterback. It seemed Tampa Bay had given up on him so quickly. It didn't make sense to me. I sat down one day to talk to James about his experience on the Buccaneers.

"James," I asked him, "when you came out of the game, in between downs, what did your quarterback coach say to you?"

James shook his head. "My quarterback coach didn't say anything to me."

I then asked him if anyone on the offensive staff had ever discussed downs and distances with him, or talked about what coverages the other team was using. His answer, again, was no. No one had said anything to him.

I asked if anyone had even addressed what coverages he should be expecting in the red zone. This was fundamental, basic information that a quarterback needs to know—but again, James admitted that no one had told him anything about these topics.

My first response was confusion. How could this be? They were putting James Harris and the entire team in a no-win situation. It just didn't square with any kind of effective coaching methodology that I knew. Of course, Tampa Bay finished at the bottom of their division every year.

Though Tampa Bay had been willing to draft James in the first round, they had apparently not been willing to let him in on the more strategic elements of the position. In my opinion, they had essentially set James up to fail and, by extension, crippled the entire team.

Dick Vermeil was our quarterback coach on the Rams, and he was not going to let an archaic set of rules determine whom we placed on the team. Instead, he sought out the very finest athletes and did everything he could to make our quarterbacks successful.

I learned a lot from Dick in those years, not just about football strategy, but also about work ethic and how to go above and beyond for the team. It was a bit of a running joke between us that, no matter how early I arrived at the office, Dick had somehow beaten me there. I even tried on a couple of occasions to get there as early as I possibly could, only to find his car already in the parking lot and Dick already at his desk. Later, I discovered that he regularly spent the night in his office, sleeping on a divan he kept there. Dick Vermeil always gave the team everything he had, and he inspired me to work just as hard.

Shortly after we started with the Rams, the team was sold to Carroll Rosenbloom, a successful businessman who had previously owned the Baltimore Colts. He had a reputation as a hands-on owner who really took care of his team, and I saw that side of him for myself one night during a team dinner.

The two leaders on the Rams were David "Deacon" Jones and Merlin Olsen, veteran players who had been a major part of the Rams's success in the past. As we were eating one night, Deacon stood up and made the announcement that Lamar Lundy, a former player, was very ill in San Diego. Deacon was asking the members of the Rams to raise funds for Lundy's care.

Deacon—along with Merlin Olsen, Roosevelt Grier, and Lamar Lundy—was part of the "Fearsome Foursome," a formidable defensive line that had made Rams history in the late 1960s and early '70s. Now one of them was in dire need of help. Lamar Lundy would battle a number of illnesses throughout his life, from cancer to Graves' disease and many other problems, but he never quit fighting, still managing to live to the age of seventy-one.

As Deacon and Merlin began to take up their collection, Carroll Rosenbloom suddenly rose out of his seat and interrupted them. "I don't want you players to worry about Lamar Lundy," he said forcefully. "Lamar will always be a Ram, and I will take care of him. I want the rest of you to concentrate on football."

Sure enough, the very next day, an ambulance went down to San Diego and brought Lamar Lundy back to Los Angeles, where he was installed in Cedar Sinai Hospital. He got top-of-the-line medical care. Carroll Rosenbloom paid for everything.

As generous as Rosenbloom could be, however, he never forgot his first goal with the Rams: winning football games. The Baltimore Colts had had enormous success during his time as owner, even winning two Super Bowls, and he aimed to get those same results from the Rams.

The problem was one of team composition and timing. When we took over the Rams, the team was mostly stocked with players who had excellent name recognition and incredible histories, but they were getting older and were mostly on the down slopes of their careers. We needed an infusion of new blood, but it would take time to find and acquire new players.

In college football, this was an easy process; we could simply go out and recruit what we needed. In the NFL, though, there were three ways one could go about accumulating players:

1. You could trade with another team for a player of your choice. This could be a tricky prospect as, obviously, no team wants to give up a great player. What you needed could wind up costing you a valuable part of your own team. It's a difficult balance to strike, and you can be assured that the other team is always looking to get the best possible deal.

2. You could sign free agents. Free agency would include any player not currently attached to another team or any player who had played out their options with another

team and had not been re-signed by that team or any other team in the league. With free agency, the choices were slightly more limited than with trading.

3. Finally, you could simply take players during the college draft. This happened once a year and, in the '60s and '70s, the draft took place in February. These days, it's done in April, which in my opinion is better timing. In the days of the winter draft, many teams missed players who turned out to be incredible on the field because the teams simply didn't have enough time to evaluate them fully. Pushing the draft into the spring allowed for more observation and a better understanding of each player.

All of these options, however, would cost us time. We needed a young crop of players who could nevertheless carry on the tradition of excellence established by older players, and we needed to get the alchemy of the team just right. The NFL, however, doesn't build a lot of extra time into its season. The Rams's win-loss record put us squarely in the middle of the pack, and Carroll Rosenbloom was not inclined to wait for us to improve.

We hadn't even really settled in with the Rams when Rosenbloom came to Coach Prothro and informed him that he was going to change the coaching staff. Naturally, this was a huge blow to Coach Prothro, who had made a big leap coming to the Rams and was as devoted as the rest of us to making the team great.

Coach Prothro wasn't going to leave without a fight, however, and he pointed out that Rosenbloom couldn't fire him because the previous owner had given Coach Prothro everything he asked for, including a clause in his contract stating that he could not be fired.

"Oh no, Coach," Rosenbloom said immediately, "I'm not going to fire you. I'm simply going to get myself another coach." He told Tommy Prothro that he was welcome to stay on as a sort of figurehead, still receiving his salary and the other benefits mentioned in his contract, but without any real power to manage the team.

Tommy Prothro was a man of high principles, and that sort of empty arrangement was anathema to him. He refused the offer and instead chose to resign, something that I think Rosenbloom expected all along.

The coaching staff from UCLA had tied their fates to Coach Prothro's and so, when Rosenbloom hired a new coach, we were also terminated. For the first time since graduating from college, I found myself without a job. June and I had been careful to save our money during the previous years, so we weren't in desperate need, but I knew that I needed to find employment.

I had a close friend who had been the head football coach at Fremont High School. He had resigned that job shortly before I left the Rams, and he had subsequently purchased a liquor store. Liquor was big business at that time, mainly because the industry was still unregulated. My friend and I were about the same age and in similar economic circumstances, so when he heard that I was looking for a new job, he reached out to me and asked if I would like to join him in his new liquor venture. His long-term goal was to own a string of liquor stores in the area. The idea sounded lucrative and relatively secure. I asked him to give me some time to think about it, however, because I wasn't sure that I wanted to leave coaching behind.

I was still weighing my options when I received a call from Tommy Prothro, who invited June and I to have dinner with him and his wife, Shirley. Of course, we accepted, and we all had a very pleasant evening together with lots of small talk. After the meal, Coach Prothro and I retired to his study to talk in private.

Tommy Prothro was hooked on two things: cigarettes and Co-ca-Cola. As soon as we reached the study, he lit up a cigarette and poured himself a Coke. As he did so, he asked me what I was planning to do if I didn't go back to coaching. I told him about the offer my friend had made, and how I was considering it.

"Liquor stores are expensive," Coach Prothro observed.

"Yes, they are," I replied.

Then he said something I wasn't expecting at all. He told me that, if this was what I really wanted to do, he would lend me the money to get started in the liquor business. He said that he felt responsible for getting me into this situation.

For a moment, I was speechless. It was true that I had followed Coach Prothro to the Rams, but I had never blamed him for any of the turns my career had taken. I had made a careful, informed choice to go to the Rams. I had enjoyed our brief time there. It wouldn't have occurred to me that Coach Prothro was in any way responsible for my current unemployment. I was bowled over by his consideration for me and his generosity.

Coach Prothro wasn't done. He asked me if I had ever heard of a person by the name of Bob Six. I couldn't say that I had. Bob Six, Coach Prothro informed me, was the owner and CEO of Continental Airlines. He was also interested in me joining the coaching staff at the University of Colorado.

Bob Six was not an alumnus of Colorado, nor was he affiliated with the school in any official way. But Continental Airlines was headquartered in Denver, and he had taken a personal interest in the local school—and their football team. Apparently, he thought that I might be a good addition to the team's coaching staff.

"I'd be happy to introduce you, if you're interested," Coach Prothro told me. I was definitely interested. I had been on the fence about leaving coaching, and this was an opportunity to see what might be available to me in the world of college football.

The very next day, I met with Bob Six, and he arranged for me to fly out to Denver to meet with the coaching staff and the athletic director at the University of Colorado. He had already briefed them about me, and our meeting went very smoothly. No contracts were signed, but I liked the school and the coaching staff. It seemed that we were all headed for an understanding about our mutual future. By the time I flew back to Los Angeles, I was thinking that this might be the next phase of my career.

I continued to forge a friendship and a professional relationship with Bob and his wife, Audrey Meadows (an actress most famous for portraying Jackie Gleason's long-suffering wife, Alice Kramden, on *The Honeymooners*). It was always a bit strange to pick up the phone and hear her voice, so familiar from countless episodes of television, on the other end of the line. Audrey was always very solicitous. She invariably checked in with June and me and the children before she scheduled meetings between Bob and me.

We talked regularly in those days about recruiting strategies and how to get the athletes that Colorado needed. The team had two heavy hitters working on their behalf: Bob Six himself and Jack Vickers of Vickers Oil. They would take the twenty best recruits in the nation, splitting them evenly down the middle, and then they would each work on recruiting their ten athletes.

Bob quickly added me to his recruiting team, and we traveled the country from Southern California to Ohio, visiting the best athletes available and getting them to commit to Colorado. As a result, the University of Colorado had a number of championship teams in those years.

When it came to securing a desirable athlete, there was almost nothing that Bob wouldn't do. I remember one case in particular when Bob had found a young man in Southern California whom he thought was perfect for the team. The two of us visited this young man in his home and met his parents, including his father, who had recently retired from the Army and was looking for a new line of work.

Sensing an opportunity, Bob told the man that he would give him a job at Continental Airlines. The catch was, the man's son had to go to Colorado University, or Bob would fire the father. Sometimes, though, a young prospect goes another way, no matter how comprehensive the recruitment. In this case, the son chose the University of California and, true to his word, Bob did indeed fire the boy's father.

That was how serious recruiting was in those days, and I do not imagine that much has changed since then. If anything, it has probably gotten even more fraught and high-stakes.

Everything seemed to be proceeding along in a predictable fashion when, once again, I was thrown a curveball. Sitting at home one day, I received a phone call from someone who identified himself as Sid Gillman. I knew the name, of course. Even in the early '70s, Sid was a successful NFL coach. He had even helmed the LA Rams for a while. In 1960, Sid Gillman became the first coach of the then-Los Angeles Chargers (now the San Diego Chargers).

"Sorry I didn't call you earlier," he said, "but I just got the job myself." I knew who Sid was, but I thought to myself, how in the world does he know who I am?

I was still trying to figure out what we were talking about when he said: "I would like very much for you to join us in Houston."

"I'm not sure I can do that," I said immediately. This was a totally unexpected opportunity, and it threw a monkey wrench into the future I had been comfortably imagining. "I think I'm going to the University of Colorado."

Sid paused for a moment. "Have you signed a contract?" he asked.

"No," I admitted. "There's no contract, but we do have a kind of unwritten agreement."

"Would you do me a favor?" Sid asked. "Would you fly to Houston and just talk to us? No strings, just give us one conversation."

I figured that one conversation couldn't hurt anything, and the idea of working in the National Football League once again was very tempting. I agreed to come out to Houston and booked my flight shortly thereafter.

In Houston, I met Sid and the rest of the staff. We discussed every element of the job, including the salary on the table. After the meeting, I went back to my hotel room and immediately called June.

"I cannot believe," I told her, "what these people are offering me to come coach here."

I told her the amount, and she was just as stunned as I had been in the meeting (though I had tried not to show my reaction.) That kind of money could make a lot of changes in our lives. Additionally, if I worked two more years in the National Football League, I would become fully vested and eligible for the NFL's generous retirement package. Two more years, and June and I would be set during our golden years.

Everything about the job seemed perfect, but one question still loomed: What would I tell Bob Six?

That idea weighed heavily on my mind all the way from Houston back to Los Angeles. I ruminated over the problem, trying to think of the perfect way to break this news.

I had seen how seriously Bob took Colorado football, and we had become friends in the short time we had known one another. I didn't want him to be angry or disappointed with me.

I was surprised, however, when I finally got Bob on the phone and explained my new situation. He hesitated for a moment. I feared the worst, but his voice, when it came over the line, was kind.

"I understand. You've got to do what's right for you," he told me. I couldn't find the words to tell him how relieved I was.

Thus, with Bob's blessing, in the spring of 1973, I became a member of the Houston Oilers football team. Once again, I was the first African-American coach in the team's history.

CHAPTER EIGHT

Bringing Up the Durden Boys

With every new job, I had the usual complement of worries about being effective and gelling with the team. The move to the Houston Oilers, however, brought up a whole new set of concerns. I would be moving my family to Texas, and it would be the first time the boys had lived anywhere other than the LA area. I knew that Houston would be a big change for all of us, but especially for my sons, who were still quite young. Life in Houston—a fast-growing Southern city with a very different cultural background—would be unlike anything the boys had experienced before.

Some things, however, would not change. Texas in general and Houston in particular had strong, sports-oriented cultures. I knew that all my young lads—each an athlete in his own right—would find that atmosphere comforting and familiar. The boys all wanted to continue pursuing their individual sports. We were a bit surprised to discover that, unlike in Los Angeles—where we could go to the local parks and sign up to participate in nearly any sport—everything in Houston was privatized and required a fee. We wanted to make sure, however, that our sons had a certain degree of continuity in their lives.

After we had gotten settled in, June and I were keeping an eye on the boys, waiting for symptoms of homesickness or culture shock. Instead, we were surprised by how well the boys seemed to be adapting to their new home. We had expected them to be surprised or confused by new elements of life in Texas, but they all appeared to be settling in nicely. We had to make a few adjustments, of course—but, for the most part, we could hardly tell that our sons had just been moved halfway across the country.

What I didn't realize, however, was that the boys were all dealing with the change of scenery in their own ways. One day, I was walking with Michael and discussing some of the activities he was pursuing at his new school when he offered up a dilemma. "Dad," he said, "I can't understand a word the coach is saying."

I almost laughed out loud. Apparently the pronounced southern drawl in Houston was totally incomprehensible to my thoroughly Californian son.

"How do you get anything done?" I asked him, amused. By now, he had been going to school and participating in sports for a few weeks and, by all accounts, he was performing well.

Michael shrugged. "I just do whatever the other kids do."

Of course, Michael eventually learned how to parse the Texan accent and probably found that life got exponentially easier as he did so.

As with many other Southern cities, school integration had been a challenge in Houston. The school districts were still struggling to make real change by the time our family arrived in the early 1970s. They were trying to resolve some of the issues by busing White teachers into Black schools and Black teachers into White schools. The racial makeup of the classes, however, remained fairly homogenous. My middle son Kevin, for example, was the only Black student in his class, though he had an African-American teacher. All of this felt very unorthodox for June and I, who had almost exclusively experienced the more diverse Los Angeles school system.

My son Kevin is in the third row, second child from the left

Despite often being one of few African Americans in school or in other situations, the boys seemed to be developing well-rounded social circles. My youngest son, Allan, was a little social butterfly, always all over the neighborhood and making new friends wherever he went.

There was a little boy about his age who lived just across the street from us and he and Allan became fast friends. One day, the two of them were playing on the living room floor while I dozed on the couch. I was half-asleep when I heard the neighbor boy say: "You know, Allan, us Jews have to stick together."

Allan didn't miss a beat. He just nodded sagely and said, "Yeah. Us Jews gotta stick together."

I knew for a fact that Allan had no idea what a Jew was, and I didn't know if the neighborhood boy did, either. I didn't know if he was Jewish, or if perhaps it was something he had overheard—or maybe he only knew it as a word for someone different? Either way, he and my son seemed to have developed a certain camaraderie, even if it was perhaps slightly misplaced.

While the boys were settling in at school and in the neighborhood, I was getting to know the Oilers and sizing them up. I could tell right off the bat that the team needed quality players for almost every position. Our head coach at that time was Bill Peterson, who had made his reputation coaching the Florida State Seminoles into a football powerhouse. His greatest asset, however, was his uncanny ability to surround himself with great assistant coaches.

The year before I came to Houston, the Oilers had been decimated with a terrible win/loss record, winning just one game all season. We desperately needed an infusion of new players, but we also needed superior coaching for our staff. Most of the other coaches were strangers to me, and I was eager to see what each of them would bring to the table.

Our general manager was Sid Gilman, a hard-charging man who tried everything he could to bring in better talent. He knew better than anyone how badly the team needed new blood, and he was working all the time to find additional players. In the mornings, on my way to practice, I would pass by Sid's office where I could see him busy reviewing films from all over the country. When I came back in the evenings, Sid would still be there, still combing films for the right player or players.

We did our pre-season workouts in the surrounding Houston area and also in Florida, looking for new talent. As the season drew closer, it was clear that, in addition to men who could get the job done, we also needed a coaching staff who could make the right use of what we had. At the time, we already had two young quarterbacks who were very much in demand. We were regularly fielding offers from other teams in the league looking to trade. We knew that, if we traded shrewdly, we might be able to get multiple promising players for one of our quarterbacks.

Finally, our general manager called us together to discuss which of the quarterbacks we would trade and which we should keep. There was much back and forth and good arguments on both sides but, ultimately, we decided to trade Lynn Dickey and keep Dan Pastorini.

We all knew that the team did not have the sheer raw talent required to be a playoff contender. If we were going to succeed, it was going to come down to superior coaching and strategizing. I was surprised and disappointed to discover that there was little oversight from the head coach and that each of the assistant coaches was more or less on his own. This was definitely not the way things had been done on other teams I'd been with. Luckily, we had great assistant coaches.

Bill Peterson had left Florida State to take the head coach job at Rice University. He had been very successful there, and the Rice Owls were generally regarded as a good football team. When he came onto the Oilers, however, he was under a bit of a cloud because of some unfortunate things that had happened with the Rice team.

A sports reporter had approached Bill wanting to do an in-depth story about the Rice Owls (a project which later became the book *Saturday's Children*), and Bill had agreed to the idea. He had even gone so far as to allow the reporter access to all of the team meetings.

During one of these meetings, right before the team was about to take the field,, one of the players abruptly announced that he refused to play. He was upset about some post-season promises that had apparently been made to him. As Bill argued with the player, it eventually came out that the young man had been paid for his participation on the team—a huge violation of the rules for college football.

Naturally, the sports reporter had observed all of this, and it went straight into the book. The book, which made it to store shelves in 1971, was not particularly complimentary to Bill, and it included the disastrous information about the paid athlete. The NCAA reviewed the information and put the Rice Owls on probation, even though Bill had already left to join the Oilers by that time.

Of course, people associated with Rice couldn't help but feel as though they had been abandoned in their time of need by the very person who had created the problem. Thus, Bill's past followed him to the Oilers, where there was a strong Rice alumni association who weren't afraid to make their grievances known. It eventually got so bad that Coach Peterson was being harassed on a daily basis and, at one point, his critics even marched on the Oilers facility.

It was safe to say that the season was off to a rocky start, but we were working through our problems and building a stronger team. We opened our season that year in New York against the Giants. Although we lost that game, it was already clear that our young team was growing and developing, a little at a time.

Things were starting to improve for us in the win/loss column, but still we were encountering behind-the-scenes problems with the coaching staff. In light of this, Sid Gillman decided to let Bill Peterson go and take over the head coaching responsibilities himself. The change seemed to relieve a lot of tension around the program and, even though we still weren't winning the majority of our games, our team was steadily improving with each game. By the end of the season, we won our last two games. I felt sure we were on the verge of turning the team around.

I wasn't completely satisfied with my experience on the Oilers, and I had been thinking seriously about whether I wanted to commit to another year. I had been coaching for quite a while at this point, and I could sense that I was at a kind of crossroads in my career.

I had also just gotten a request from Howard University in Washington, DC asking me to fly in and interview to become the head football coach there. Head coach would definitely be a step up and, even though I had been rethinking coaching in general, I believed I should at least follow up on the offer.

While I was there, however, nine inches of snow fell, and that pretty much made up my mind. I didn't want to live on the East Coast. As I headed back to Houston, I was unsure about my future, but I knew that, just as East Coast wasn't for me and my family, neither were we Texans. One way or another, I felt sure that we would soon be returning home to Los Angeles.

I kept these thoughts to myself, however, and didn't discuss them with anyone but my wife. As the end of the season was approaching, I knew I would have to make a decision one way or another. Nearly every day, I would see Coach Gillman in the hall and he would encourage me to come into his office so we could sign a new contract for the following year. I was able to put him off for a little while but, eventually, I had to bite the bullet.

One night, I told June that I was going to tell Sid I wasn't going to sign another contract because we were going back to LA. My plan at this point was to leave coaching and go into a more rooted business, in a place where the family could settle down. The boys were at a point where they needed consistency in their lives.

I thought I would follow up with my friend about his liquor business. It was still a very lucrative business, especially as we had talked about purchasing a chain of liquor stores. We even planned to secure a parcel of land where we could store the liquor until it was distributed to our retail outlets. In those days, hard liquor could only be sold at specific liquor outlets. It was very different from today, when you can find a liquor aisle in virtually every supermarket! I felt it would be a nice, steady business that would allow us to stay in one place so the boys could complete school while still providing enough income to take care of everyone.

The following day—a Wednesday—I headed to Sid's office and told him that I would not be returning for another year on the Houston Oilers. For a moment, he looked shocked. I thought he might have had a sense of how ambivalent I was about extending my contract, but apparently, it was coming as a surprise to him.

Then he looked up at me and said simply, "Okay. You're terminated as of Friday."

And that was all he had to say about the matter.

I went home and told June how the meeting had gone, and she began preparations for our departure. We had already started contacting real estate agents and were planning to sell our home in Houston. Then, before we had time to make any more plans, I received a phone call from Coach Prothro.

"Earnel," he said, "it hasn't been released to the press yet, but I've taken the job as head coach on the San Diego Chargers. I would very much like to have you join me there."

Even though I had been so close to leaving coaching behind, I couldn't say no. I told June when I got off the phone that, if it had been anyone else in the world but Tommy Prothro, I wouldn't have taken the job.

I knew that June had been looking forward to returning to Los Angeles, so I assured her that we would only go to San Diego for two or three years at the most and then we would go back home, to the five bedroom house in LA that we were currently leasing out. It did feel good to be heading back to Southern California, at least.

In the spring of '74, I joined Coach Prothro on the San Diego

Chargers. June stayed behind in Houston to sell our house there and also to allow the boys to finish out the school year. On weekends, she would fly out to San Diego to look for housing. We had discussed neighborhoods where we wanted to buy and eventually agreed that the La Mesa area would probably be best for us.

During my recruiting seasons at UCLA, our coaches had discovered a few school districts in the San Diego area where a great emphasis was placed on both athletics and academics. We found that students from two schools in particular—Kearney High School and Helix High School—seemed to fit in well at UCLA. The transition from high school athlete to college athlete seemed to go a bit more smoothly for them. In those days, Kearny ruled the football landscape in San Diego, but my first choice for the boys was Helix High.

Our Houston home sold quickly and, before we knew it, June and boys were settling into our La Mesa house. We didn't waste any time getting the boys enrolled in school. Michael was headed into ninth grade at Helix High School and Kevin was going to La Mesa Middle School while Allan attended La Mesa Dale Elementary School.

Michael was nearly fifteen years old by this time, and he had developed into a fine athlete. He was handsome and tall and talented at a number of sports, everything a parent could wish for in a son. We wanted to make sure, however, that Michael paid as much attention to his academics as he did to sports. He was entering high school, and we knew that his academic performance would only become more important as he grew older.

Before Michael started school, we had prepared a list of classes that we wanted him to enroll in, based on courses he'd previously taken in Houston and LA. However, when Michael brought this list of classes to the counselor who was supposed to help him get his schedule in order, she dismissed them out of hand.

"You don't need these courses," she said, "because you're not going to college anyway."

Michael was nonplussed by this but, as a young teenager in a brand new school, he wasn't prepared to contradict a person in a position of authority. That night when I asked him how his class schedule had shaken out, he told me the whole story.

I have rarely ever been so angry. How dare this person—a total stranger—tell my son what his life and career would hold? She had spent just a few seconds with Michael, and yet nevertheless felt that she knew everything about his future.

The next morning, I marched directly down to the school as soon as they opened their doors and demanded to speak to the counselor. I was told that she "wasn't available," but I certainly didn't intend to leave without seeing her. I told the receptionist that I wasn't going anywhere until I saw either the counselor or the principal.

By this time, the principal—Dr. King—had heard the commotion and had emerged from his office to see what was going on. He beckoned me into his office and asked me what had happened. I explained the whole story to him and he immediately apologized for the counselor's behavior, assuring me that Michael would get his classes.

Dr. King was as good as his word and, over the months and years, we actually became very good friends. We're still good friends, in fact, and neither Michael nor his brothers had any further problems with taking whatever courses they chose.

It was track season when Michael started at Helix, so he immediately went out for the team. It didn't take long for him to start distinguishing himself on the track. People around campus quickly began to realize that Michael was a special athlete, winning nearly every event he entered. When he was still just a ninth grader, Michael won the league's 200-meter dash and took second in the

100-meter dash. He also anchored the two relay teams, the 4 by 100 and the 4 by 400. Heads were turning all over town.

Michael specialized in the 400 meters. During his four years at Helix, he never lost a race in the 400 meters in the Grossmont League. But his first love was always basketball, and he was just as good on the court as he was on the track. For a long time, he was the only ninth grader in the history of the school to ever win a varsity letter. This was quite a feat when you think about some of Helix's other graduates, people like Bill Walton and Wilbert Orlandi, both of whom went on to UCLA and then to the NBA.

Despite being the son of a football coach, Michael didn't actually add football to his repertoire until his junior year, when he promptly became the Grossmont League's best receiver. By his senior year, he was the league all-time quarterback.

Helix went to the playoffs that year, thus kicking off a string of playoff appearances that has lasted until this day. In Michael's senior year, the Grossmont League did well in the playoffs, until they met Kearney High School. In those days, Kearney was the best team in San Diego County, and Helix High just couldn't overcome them.

The Helix/Kearney game was hotly anticipated in San Diego and beyond. Recruiters from schools around the country came to that game to scout the athletes. Later, a UCLA recruiter told me that Colorado and some other schools had come specifically to recruit Michael, because they had been watching his high school career for a long time. The game against Kearney sealed the deal for UCLA, even though Helix lost.

As it turned out, Michael's erstwhile "counselor" couldn't have been more wrong about his college prospects. When his senior year came, he had several options to choose from. Eventually, he chose to go to UCLA, a decision I wholeheartedly supported. In the fall of 1979, he headed off for Los Angeles, ready to begin the next phase of his academic and athletic career.

Michael had set an excellent example for his younger brothers. Not only had he distinguished himself as an athlete but he had also maintained a high academic standard and earned himself a scholarship to one of the finest universities in the land.

Neither Kevin nor Allan had Michael's height or his natural speed, but they were fine athletes in their own right. After finishing at La Mesa Middle School, Kevin went on to Helix, ready to pick up where Michael had left off. Kevin didn't play basketball, but he played football and ran track, and he did well in both sports. During Kevin's junior year, his team won the CIF (California Interscholastic Federation) championship, beating San Pasquale High School at Qualcomm Stadium in San Diego, which became one of the major highlights of his high school football career.

The next year, Allan joined his brother at Helix. For a while, it seemed like the Durden family was dominating high school athletics in San Diego. In 1983, the Helix High football team went undefeated and was noted as one of the best high school teams in the nation, in part because of the contributions of Allan and Kevin. To this day, Michael and Allan both still have records on the books at Helix. It seemed that everywhere you turned in those days, there was a Durden setting records and winning championships. You can bet your life that I was one proud papa.

Both Kevin and Allan attracted a lot of attention from recruiters and, like Michael, they more or less had their pick of a number of good schools. Kevin finally settled on Idaho State while Allan chose the University of Arizona.

I had promised all of my sons that, if they got a scholarship for the college or university they attended, I would buy each of them a new automobile upon their graduation from high school. As it turned out, each of my lads drove brand new cars to the colleges of their choice.

When Michael was a senior at UCLA and Allan was a freshman at Arizona, the two of them actually played one another at the Rose Bowl Stadium in Pasadena. June and I attended the game. It was the first time that I had been to the Rose Bowl stadium since I had played there myself in 1957. Fortunately for June and I, the game was a tie.

When Michael graduated from UCLA, he was taken by the San Francisco 49ers in the college draft.

With son Mike, when he played for the 49ers

After a couple of years, he went up to Canada and played for the Edmonton Eskimos for a few seasons. Around that time, he received a very lucrative offer from the New York Jets. He called me one day to ask if we could meet and discuss his next move. Of course I said yes.

Michael told me that football had been good to him. It had facilitated his education at a top-tier school and it had paid him well enough to create a nice nest egg. Nevertheless, he had started to feel that he'd had enough of football, and he didn't want to accept the Jets's offer, attractive though it was.

It seemed to me that his decision was already mostly made. I wondered if he had wanted to meet with me to get my approval for this choice. Michael had always known how important athletics were for me, but I loved my children for all that they were, and no one part of them was any more important than the others. I told Michael that there was indeed life after football, and I advised him to write the Jets and inform them of his decision.

Michael walked away from football that day and he never looked back. I knew that whatever he chose to do next, I would be proud of him. Careers in professional sports are often much shorter than those in more traditional lines of work. I knew that, for each of my sons, there would come a day when the benefits of the sport no longer outweighed the challenges.

While Michael was making his way in the NFL, Kevin and Allan were starting their college careers at their respective universities. One day during practice, Kevin got his foot caught on the Astroturf and came away with torn ligaments in his knee. He elected to come back home to San Diego to do his rehabilitation. During that time, he decided not to return to Idaho State, and instead enrolled at Cal State Fullerton. Even after his knee had healed, Kevin was never quite the same athletically. I knew from my own experiences with a significant injury how demoralizing it could be, and I believed that Kevin had simply lost his passion for the game.

Meanwhile, Allan —one of the finest receivers in San Diego County history—was being switched to defensive back while playing for the University of Arizona. I objected profusely, but Allan himself didn't seem to mind, at least at first, because his new position would make him an instant starter on defense.

Allan was the smallest of the three boys, but I believe that he might have been the most tenacious. He was always a fierce competitor because, lacking some of the natural advantages of a larger player, he had to be. He didn't have the speed of his older brother Mike, but he worked hard to become a fine hurdler, and he ran whatever events the coach wanted him to run. Allan was also a good basketball player, having played on the well-regarded Helix team, and he always seemed to excel in whatever events he chose. Allan grew into a fine athlete at Helix and later at the University of Arizona, and soon he was respected throughout the PAC-10.

Coach Terry Donahue of UCLA once said he had made a big mistake by not recruiting Allan harder when he was coming out of high school. After a game against California, Arizona's defensive back coach, Moe Ankney, commented that, although Allan was the smallest defensive back, he was a smart player and very quick. He said, "The Durden speed and techniques also helped him block a punt against Stanford," for which his coaches later gave him defensive player honor.

On September, 22, 1982, Arizona played LSU. Allan had a fine game, leading head coach Larry Smith to say, "Our free safety Allan Durden's high school experience as a wide receiver helped him recognize the pass pattern and react quickly to the ball on his school record, a ninety-six yard interception for a touchdown."

Bill Nixon of the *Phoenix Gazette* wrote about Allan saying that, "At first he was a little perturbed about changing his position from wide receiver to defensive back. After, he came to Tucson with top credentials: 83 receptions, 109 yards, and 17 touchdowns in his last two seasons at La Mesa." Nixon wrote that Allan "carried a 3.2 GPA into his junior year in 1984. After four games in 1984, one might wonder what the 5'11", 167-pound athlete could do for an encore?" On the Wildcats, Allan once again found himself one of the smallest players, just as he had been the smallest boy in the Durden household. And, once again, he had compensated by giving the game everything he had and proving his durability time and time again.

Allan went on to make the Walter Camp All-American team as defensive back and was taken by the Detroit Lions in the college draft. After a while, he was traded to the Buffalo Bills, and then he came back home to the San Diego Chargers. By this time, he was pretty well beat up and decided to call it a day as far as professional football was concerned.

I couldn't have been prouder of my sons. Each of them spent years working to accomplish their dreams and, no matter when they chose in the remainder of their individual careers, they did it on their own terms and in their own time.

CHAPTER NINE

Rebuilding the Chargers and Saying Goodbye

While the boys were making their mark on Helix High School and the world at large, I was hard at work with Coach Prothro on the San Diego Chargers. In the beginning, our biggest problems were rebuilding the team after years of disappointing performances and mediocre AFC West placements and also getting out from under a reputation for drug usage.

In the 1970s, drug use was rampant in the National Football League. Two major classes of drugs—amphetamines for "energy" and steroids for size—were woven into the fabric of the game. The Chargers were hardly the only team to indulge, but an investigatory probe by the league soon identified a large number of players abusing dangerous prescription medications. Nearly all of these drugs were provided by the team doctor, Arnold Mandell.

It was this scandal that had pushed previous head coach Harland Svare to step down and allowed Tommy Prothro to take his place. Coach Prothro wanted to make sure that no taint remained from the previous years, so he immediately purged anyone on the team associated with the drug scandal, including Dr. Mandell.

We were left with a roster full of more junior players, including Dan Fouts, a young quarterback from the University of Oregon.

We struggled through our first full season in 1974, limping along with a young team that had been recently driven by high-profile turmoil. It was clear to the entire coaching staff that, if we wanted to be competitive in the next season, we would need to find new, effective additions to the team.

With this in mind, Coach Prothro decided to stage an all-out recruiting effort in advance of the '75 season. He divided his coaching staff into three groups; the first would head south and review the teams down there, the second would go east to do the same thing, and the third would travel west. I was in the first group, headed for the south. We considered ourselves the lucky ones because we had access to team owner Eugene Kline's private airplane, which meant we could come and go as we pleased.

The southern group was filled out with John David Crowe, offensive coordinator; Jackie Simpson, defensive coordinator; Bob Kittrick, offensive line coach; Harland Svare general manager; Tommy Prothro, head coach; and, of course, me as the offensive back coach. The rest of our staff and scouts were split evenly amongst the other two groups.

We left San Diego the day after Christmas and we were on the road for two weeks. Our first stop was Houston, then Florida, and then Louisiana before we headed on to Mississippi, Alabama, Arkansas, and Tennessee. Everyplace we stayed, we each had our own rooms complete with projectors and films of all the athletes we were evaluating. Each player was graded as an athlete on a scale of one to ten, with Coach Prothro having the final say on each prospect.

We had a lot of work to do and only about two weeks to do it in, so everyone on the coaching staff had to work as much as possible. Once we settled into our rooms in front of those films, we didn't leave again until it was time to move on to the next city. Even our food was brought to us. There were times when I had no idea whether it was night or day because I hadn't been outside for so long. We evaluated players all day long and then, eventually, the word would come down: "Be prepared to close down and move out in fifteen or twenty minutes."

They were absolutely serious about those fifteen or twenty minutes, too. We usually had just enough time to gather up our few belongings and get out the door before we were on the road again. This was where Eugene Kline's plane came in handy. We could leave whenever we pleased, night or day, and we were able to see more cities overall. We had cast our net widely, looking at any player who had any potential whatsoever. The more cities we could visit, the more practices we could look in on, and the more players we could see, the better the odds of finding that one gem amidst all the others who didn't make the cut.

In 1975, we had two number one draft picks and two number two picks. Our first draft pick was Gary "Big Hands" Johnson a defensive end out of Grambling State University in Louisiana. The second of our number one draft picks was Mike Williams, a LSU defensive back. For our number two picks, we selected Louie Kelcher, a SMU defensive tackle, and Fred Dean, a linebacker from Louisiana Tech. These players would become the cornerstone of our defense for the next six years.

Despite our recruiting efforts, the 1975 Charger team did not do very well in terms of a win-loss record. However, we had expected that this would be an "educational" season, and we could see that the team was gaining invaluable experience. We had expected that this would be the case because we had recruited a large number of quite young players, knowing that they would grow faster with on-the-field experience.

Over the course of the season, it became clear that we were having some consistent problems with our offensive unit. Coach Prothro set out to remedy the issue. His best solution came in the form of new assistant coach, Bill Walsh. I had heard much about Bill and his successes, especially in the training of quarterbacks, and I knew I wasn't the only one on the Chargers who was eager to see what he would bring to the team.

During his time with the Cincinnati Bengals as a quarterback and receiver coach, Bill Walsh had consistently kept their offense amongst the best in the NFL. He was also a generous and thoughtful person, and we became good friends almost immediately.

Bill's most important project, as he saw it, was to deal with our young quarterback, Dan Fouts. In February 1976, Bill got to work in earnest developing Fouts's skills. I was very curious about Bill's process, so I tagged along on their sessions in the hopes of finding out how Bill had developed so many great quarterbacks. Every single quarterback that Bill had ever coached was in the Football Hall of Fame in Canton, Ohio. Clearly, he was doing something right. I wanted to find out what exactly that was.

The San Diego Chargers Football Coaches in 1976. Bottom row, from left to right: Bill Walsh, Howard Mudd, Bob McKittrick, Earnel Durden. Top row from left to right, Ernie Zampese, Tommy Prothro, Jackie Simpson, Rudy Feldman

For the first few sessions, neither he nor Fouts touched a football. Instead, he worked on disconnecting from the center. Anyone who watches football regularly has probably seen a quarterback get their feet entangled with the pulling guards or with some other linemen. Bill's approach was to avoid this issue by taking a big first step back, which he called the "disconnect step."

Once this was established, he worked with Fouts on opening his hips and pointing his foot where he wanted to throw the ball. Bill showed Fouts the steps necessary for throwing certain passes: three steps for short passes, five steps for medium passes, seven steps for long passes. He emphasized looking down the field and suddenly turning toward the target. Dan Fouts was right-handed, so Bill had Dan open to his right all the time, sometimes looking at the right corner and opening quickly before throwing the ball to the left side.

One day, as we were all coming off of the field, I asked Bill why he concentrated so much on the left cornerback. He answered me by directing me to stand over on the right side, as though I were the right cornerback. As the quarterback disconnected from the center, he asked me: "What do you see?"

"I see the ball," I said.

"Exactly," Bill answered. "We want to take advantage of the guy who doesn't see the ball, the left corner." That made a lot of sense to me, though it was not something I had ever thought of before. This was just one of many things that I would learn from Bill during these sessions with Fouts.

As for Dan Fouts himself, the rest is history. He went on to be one of the best quarterbacks of his time. For the next five years, our offense was the best in the NFL and Fouts, just like the rest of Bill's quarterbacks, also ended up in the Hall of Fame.

When I brought my family to San Diego, I was fully expecting to stay with the team for a few seasons and then head back to Los

Angeles. Instead, I spent fourteen amazing years with the Chargers, and we never did make it back to LA. Eventually, we sold our property in Del Amo Woods, making San Diego our only home.

The coaches in 1977. The top row from left to right, Bob McKittrick, Head Coach Tommy Prothro, Earnel Durden, Max Coley. Bottom row from left to right, Rudy Feldman, Jackie Simpson, Larry Weaver, Jerry Smith

During those fourteen years, I had the invaluable opportunity to work closely with giants of the field like Tommy Prothro, Don Coryell, Dick Vermeil, Bill Walsh, Ernie Zampese, Joe Gibbs, and countless others. These were truly standout moments in my career that I will always remember.

Earnel Durden, Don Coryell, Dave Levy with the San Diego Chargers

Our Chargers team of 1979, '80, and '81 was an NFL championship team, and we frequently lit up the scoreboards with thirty to forty points a game. We were known as a passing team, with Dan Fouts throwing the ball to the likes of Kellen Winslow, Charlie Joiner, Wes Chandler, Eric Sievers, and Pete Holohan.

We figured that we could score anywhere and we could—and did—strike anywhere on the field. Though we were best known for passing, we were also capable of running the ball with great success, with the likes of Chuck Muncie, Ricky Bell, James Brooks, John Cappelletti, and Clarence Williams carrying the ball. We came to be respected in the air as well as on the ground.

Me coaching Chuck Muncie

During my decade and a half with the team, there were a great many games that stand out in my memory. Games like the Monday night match against the world champion Pittsburgh Steelers. We came into that one the underdog by a wide margin, but when it was all over, we had run away with the game. There was also the "Holy Roller," a game that changed the landscape of pro-football where we faced off against the Oakland Raiders and a last-minute fumble by the Raiders won them the game. That matchup is still hotly debated to this day and was the direct cause of an amendment to the league's rules.

Perhaps the most memorable game, however, was our 1982 playoff game against the Miami Dolphins, which we won, 41 to 38. Later, the media would call it the greatest game in the National Football League history.

Miami that day was so incredibly hot and humid that the Orange Bowl was like one enormous outdoor sauna. Just walking around outside was like having warm, wet blankets draped all over your body. Nevertheless, we opened with a 24 to nothing lead in the first half before Miami rallied to tie the game.

The *New York Times* called it, "The ... wildest, highest-scoring playoff game in the NFL." Our victory there would send us to the American Conference Championship for the second year in a row.

But it certainly didn't come easy for us.

On that day, our players gave all that they had and then some. Kellen Winslow was one of the biggest heroes of that day, and Miami coach Don Shula wasn't exaggerating when he called him "Superman." Kellen caught thirteen passes for 166 yards that day, although perhaps his finest hour came near the end of the regulation game.

By the end of the fourth quarter, all of his heroics had taken a toll upon Kellen Winslow. Heat and dehydration had him cramping up wildly, especially in his thighs and calves. He could barely make it to the bench, hobbling painfully and trying not to vomit. No one in the world could have faulted him for ending his game right there—but that's not what Winslow did.

The Dolphins were preparing to attempt a forty-three-yard field goal that surely would have won them the game. Kellen Winslow was determined to stop them. His teammates objected when he dragged himself to his feet—he could barely walk, let alone get the kind of height he would need to touch a ball in mid-air.

But Winslow refused to stay on the bench. He must have known that, somewhere buried deep, he had a few more ounces of energy. He called upon all his fortitude as the kick sailed overhead, launching himself as high as he could go. At 6'6" and more than 250 pounds, Winslow wasn't exactly made for high jumping under ordinary circumstances. At that moment, every muscle in his body must have been screaming in pain. But luck was on our side, because the kick was just slightly lower than usual and Winslow made it just high enough to tap the ball with his fingertips. It wasn't much, but it was enough to change the trajectory of the ball and ensure that the kick went wide.

We were still in the game and the game was headed into overtime.

Kellen paid for his exertions. He collapsed immediately after his jump and had to be helped off the field, his muscles jittering and spasming wildly. We would find out later that his body temperature had spiked to an incredible 105 degrees and he had lost thirteen pounds in water weight over the course of the game.

Winslow wasn't the only one hurting, however. The heat and humidity—as well as the incredible tension—had taken its toll on everyone. The thought of playing an overtime period was almost physically painful. And yet, that's exactly what the team had to do.

Even in overtime, the game was incredibly hard fought. We all felt the blow when placekicker Rolf Benirschke went wide with a 27-yard kick early in the overtime period. So, when Fouts was able to get the team 39 yards down the middle of the field to Miami's ten yard line, setting Benirschke up for a 29-yard kick, our hearts were in our throats.

One minute and eight seconds left in overtime and Benirschke's kick soared, a perfect arc this time, right through the waiting up-rights. We had won, 41 to 38, and the game had lasted a grueling four hours and forty-five minutes.

Kellen Winslow was not the only player who was left battered and depleted after the Miami game. Our team as a whole was completely sapped of strength. Though we were obviously happy to have won, there was very little of the usual boisterous celebration that usually accompanied a victory. Instead, it seemed that everyone was simply struggling to stay upright and conscious.

On the flight back home to San Diego, the plane was completely silent. As I walked up and down the aisle, it seemed that everyone had lapsed into a deep sleep—and not just the players, either. Of course, the coaches didn't have the added physical stress of playing the game—but even just walking the sidelines during the game had left us wringing wet in the overpowering heat. Everyone was dehydrated and sore, worn out mentally and physically.

When the plane landed in San Diego, the players could hardly even make it to the waiting bus that would take them back to the stadium. Though it was two in the morning when we arrived at the stadium, there was a small crowd of mostly family members waiting to welcome us home. The players leaned on friends and family members to make their way slowly to the waiting cars.

Our usual post-game routine was to meet on Monday to review the film of the game we had played on the previous Sunday and make appropriate corrections. After the meeting, the players would go out on to the field and jog a bit, just to get loose and work out some of the knots. On this particular Monday, though, it was obvious that our players were still feeling the effects of the Miami game. Everyone seemed listless and walked around as if in a daze. It was clear to me that their bodies had not yet recovered from playing an aggressive game in a veritable sauna the day before.

Our players took the rest of that Monday off, as usual, and the following Tuesday as well, returning on Wednesday to make preparations for our next game that Sunday. In this case, we were headed to Cincinnati to play the Bengals for the AFC championship. It was a hugely important game—but already, there were signs of trouble.

All week, we had been hearing about the extreme weather conditions in Cincinnati. We knew it would be cold, but it was much worse than anyone expected. It was so cold, in fact, that this game was destined to be known as the "Freeze Bowl," the coldest game ever played in the history of the NFL.

When we arrived in Cincinnati on Friday, the temperature was already hovering around zero degrees. By game day, it had dipped to 9 degrees below zero. With the wind chill factor, the air dropped to a painful -59 degrees out on the field. Instead of leaping from the frying pan into the fire, we had leapt from the fire to the Arctic tundra.

Just before the game started, I walked out onto the field, turning back three times to adjust my clothing in the face of the piercing wind. After struggling through even a short walk in those conditions, I wondered how I was going to last on the sidelines for an entire two-hour game. As I stood there, Wes Chandler approached and asked, "Coach? Can I go inside? My hands are frozen."

He held them up for me, and I could tell by his movements that they were stiff and painful. It was then that I realized exactly how much trouble we were in. At heart, we were a passing team—and if Wes's hands were frozen before the game had even begun, I could only imagine how Dan Fouts and the receivers were doing.

This would have been a difficult game even under the best circumstances because the team was still physically reeling from their exertions in Miami. I began to wonder if we hadn't played our Super Bowl there at the Orange Bowl.

To this day, I believe that the people of Cincinnati did not see the real Chargers at their best, the way the crowd in Miami had. I know our team gave everything they had against the Bengals. But on that day, under those circumstances, it simply was what it was.

We lost that game 27 to 7, but it was not due to a lack of effort and certainly not a lack of heart. To me, that Chargers team was as fine a group of young men as I have ever been associated with.

The 1982 Chargers season was a disappointment—we finished seventh in the AFC West division. It was our first losing season in seven years (though we did lead the NFL in passing for our sixth consecutive year in 1982, something that remains an NFL record). The 1983 season found us trying to improve upon our disappointing 6–3 record in '82, which we did, ending the '83 season with a 6–10 record. It was an improvement, but we still had a lot of work to do.

In 1985, San Diego finished with an 8 and 8 record, fourth in the AFC division. We had improved our offense considerably—but for some reason, our defense just couldn't seem to catch up. We struggled during those seasons, and the strain between the coaching staff and the team owner started to show.

Early in 1986, right after the completion of the '85 season, head coach Don Coryell and the team's owner, Alex Spanos, had some very serious discussions about how the team should be managed. Rumors had been circulating all year that Mr. Spanos was not happy with the way Coach Coryell was running the team. Some even speculated that Spanos wanted the team to be run more like a business. But Don Coryell was a coach, not a businessman.

We had also heard that Spanos already had his choice for Coryell's replacement picked out: Al Saunders, our wide-receiver coach. Spanos allegedly wanted a younger man at the helm, and Saunders was certainly young; he had only been coaching in the NFL for four years at that time.

I don't know exactly what happened during those meetings between Spanos and Coryell, but soon, Coryell left the Chargers organization, never to return. Almost immediately, it was all but confirmed that Al Saunders would be taking over the position. Some of us couldn't help but wonder if Al was the best choice, given his relatively limited experience. As it turned out, Saunders would only last two years with the Chargers, and he left the organization in bad shape.

This was far from the first administrative shakeup I'd witnessed during my time in professional football, but it was, I realized, possibly my last. I had started to get tired of seeing the same patterns over and over played out with different coaches and different owners but no meaningful change in the overall policy.

As I mulled over possibly leaving the Chargers—and the sport—my mind began to wander over the whole of my career. Some people say that, when someone is dying, their life flashes before their eyes. I suppose, in some ways, a part of my life was dying then, and my history with football was flashing before me.

I thought about my coaching and teaching years and my college days. I remembered all the way back to high school. But I kept returning, again and again, to one particular memory from the summer of 1965. That year, I had decided to teach summer school, after having attended summer school myself the previous year to amass credits and increase my teaching salary.

That summer was drawing to a close. It was mid-August, and my thoughts had mostly been consumed by the upcoming school year and my own teaching plans. I had heard, however, about an impending confrontation between police and the residents of Watts, a community in South Los Angeles that was predominantly Black.

Watts, along with its neighbor, Compton, was one of the few places that African Americans were allowed to buy or rent property in Los Angeles, leading to explicitly "Black" and "White" neighborhoods. Unsurprisingly, African-American neighborhoods like Watts were offered uniformly inferior public services (like schools and transportation) and were heavily policed by an LAPD, a force known for its brutality. People in Watts were restricted in terms of where they could live, the kinds of jobs they could have, and even where they could safely travel in the city.

By 1965, tensions were high. When a young Watts man was arrested for driving while intoxicated, sparking a violent interaction with police, it seemed that the dam had finally burst. Word filtered out to the rest of Los Angeles slowly. At first, we didn't realize the true scope of what was happening.

That day, after my summer school classes were over, I got into my car and headed home. I knew the general outlines of what was happening in Watts, but I didn't know any specifics and I was curious, so I decided to drive down Compton Boulevard rather than taking my usual way home. As I crossed El Segundo and Compton Boulevard, I was confronted with a sight that I never could have imagined in the city where I had spent most of my youth.

It looked more like the set of a war movie than a small community. There were cars abandoned the side of the road, burning unchecked. Smoke rose up and obscured everything. I could smell it even inside my vehicle. As I crossed 130th Street and Compton Boulevard, I saw people running everywhere and anywhere. They were screaming, panicked, and didn't seem to know what to do or where to go.

Suddenly, I noticed a police car rolling up behind me with lights flashing. As I pulled over to the curb and stopped, I was acutely aware of the potentially dangerous situation I had put myself in. I did not live in Watts and I was not a participant on either side of this conflict, but I knew that, in this situation, my skin color would probably tell a White police officer everything he needed to know.

I took a nervous look back at the cruiser, only to see a familiar face as my friend, Art Rundals, stepped out from the police vehicle. At the time, I still owned a duplex on Manhattan Place. I lived in one apartment and Art Rundals and his family occupied the other. Art was a deputy sheriff with Los Angeles County at the time. I didn't realize it then, but several other law enforcement agencies had been called in to quell the riots.

Art walked up to the car and asked, "Earnel, what are you doing here?"

I told him that I was on my way home from summer school. "But this is no place to be right now," I admitted.

"Follow close behind me," Art said, "and I'll get you out of here."

Art flipped on his siren and began to weave through the crowded streets with me following close behind. It was remarkable to me how tightly contained the violence and confusion was. After just a few streets, we were back in the LA that I recognized, in a neighborhood that was placid and unremarkable. The City of Los Angeles had done everything it could to tuck its Black residents into small pockets of land and confine them there. Now their resistance was also apparently confined to that tiny geographic area.

I rushed home immediately to tell June what was happening and what I had witnessed. That was the first day of the Watts riots. Things would get far worse before the violence ceased.

I think I came back to that experience so often because it was indelible. I could not have forgotten it even if I had wanted to; that day, it felt like I had wandered into the end of the world. At the time, I think we all imagined that it was the end of a certain kind of world—the end of a world where the city's Black residents accepted housing and job discrimination, a hostile police force, and depleted community services without protest. The residents of Watts had been backed into a corner—quite literally in the case of many residents who were largely barred from other, more suburban or more explicitly White neighborhoods in Los Angeles. They had made their frustration and pain clear.

It seemed to me that, after what had happened in Watts, we could not continue to pretend that African Americans were afforded the same rights and privileges as White Americans. The country could not ignore the way institutions systemically placed Black people and communities subordinate to the needs of White people and communities. How could anyone have seen what I saw that day and not realized that something had to change?

The Watts riots were just one part of the Civil Rights movement, and I watched with interest as great changes swept over the country. I had always believed that things were slowly but surely improving for Black players and coaches in professional football. I knew it wasn't the same as dismantling housing discrimination or Jim Crow segregation, but I always believed that I and other people of color working in professional football were making a difference. We were demonstrating, day after day, that Black players and coaches could make positive contributions to the game, and that we had so much more to offer than the traditional, limited roles we had been assigned.

When Dan Coryell left the Chargers, however, I was apparently not even considered for the head coaching position. I started to question what I'd really been doing all of these years. It wasn't just that I had been passed over for the promotion. It wasn't just that the job had been offered to a young coach with only four years of experience. It was the fact that no one raised even the slightest objection to this. Not one person suggested that Saunders might not be the only—or best—option. Nobody pointed out the fact that I had given the Chargers thirteen years of dedicated service. The fact that no one even considered me for the job was, apparently, completely normal and expected.

As I looked around at the professional football industry, I couldn't deny that my situation was indeed "business as usual." No team in the National Football League had ever had an African-American head coach. I had been coaching at the professional level for seventeen years and at the college level for seven. It seemed that my work—and the work of countless others—had done nothing to crack the ceiling on achievement for Black coaches.

After Saunders's uncontested appointment to head coach, I was angry—but even more than that, I was disillusioned. I wasn't sure that I wanted to go on being an assistant coach. I realized that, if I wasn't offered a head coaching job with the Chargers, I probably wasn't going to be offered a head coaching job anywhere. Perhaps I had risen as high as I could in professional football. I wasn't sure I wanted to keep working toward a goal that might be impossible.

I knew I couldn't stay with the Chargers—my feelings were just too raw. So I walked away in 1987. There was some interest from the Kansas City Chiefs and the Cincinnati Bengals, but the conversations failed to progress. More than anything else, though, I was tired. I had given decades of my life to football, and now I felt ready to take some time to be with my family and relax before starting the next phase of my life.

CHAPTER TEN

Life After Coaching

That summer, I thought constantly about my next move. Now that I had left professional football behind, it seemed that, as the summer days stretched out, my thoughts expanded with them. I briefly considered dozens of jobs, some sensible, some very unlikely. The truth was, I could do just about anything I chose—and that made choosing even harder.

I wasn't worried about my family financially. We had always done well in that department, and June and I had been careful to plan and save for the future. My next career move wouldn't be about money so much as finding something interesting and useful to occupy my time. I knew myself well enough to know that I would quickly get bored if I didn't have something challenging to tackle. After all, even when I was coaching, I had also dabbled in real estate. I'd tried radio station ownership and I'd even thought about getting involved in a golf learning center with a company out of Canada. Along with Kellan Winslow, I'd invested in a small computer company, and I was always on the lookout for interesting opportunities. So the idea of just accepting an early retirement and sitting around the house was absolutely not an option for me.

Meanwhile, my wife June had been exploring her own business ventures. As the boys grew up and headed off to high school and college, June had gotten more and more interested in becoming an entrepreneur. She had been involved in the campaign to promote Dick Gregory's Bahamian Diet products, but her biggest project was building a maid service from the ground up. Her goal was to develop and promote her company and then launch it in the San Diego area. Ideally, it would pick up steam and break into other areas, and she could begin franchising the business.

To help her develop the business, she hired the gentleman who had organized and franchised the Red Carpet Real Estate Company. She also contracted the Merry Maids Company (who were, at the time, the best maid service in the country) to come to San Diego and train her maids.

I just watched proudly as June transformed herself into a small business owner. Once in a while, she would ask for my opinion on some element of the business—but there was no question about who was in charge!

As we were navigating our own career transitions, there were even bigger changes afoot for the Durden family. Michael and Kevin, our older sons, had both been married for a few years, but it was their younger brother Allan, however, who called us one day to inform us that we were soon to be grandparents.

Our grandson's expectant mother was a young lady named Julie Olsen, whom Allan had met while at the University of Arizona. Julie was—and is—a beautiful young woman whom we love very much, to this day. She and Allan decided not to stay together as a couple, but they maintained a friendly and caring relationship as they prepared to parent their son together.

When the baby was born, they named him Ryan Dale Durden, and he was indeed the apple of our eye. He grew up traveling between Tucson, Arizona and San Diego, spending time with both sides of his loving family. Over the years, we watched as Ryan grew into a handsome and good-hearted young man.

Meanwhile, Michael and his wife had also begun to have children, first a son and then a daughter. They named their son Eric Earnel Durden and their daughter Lisa Marie Durden. Naturally, I was very pleased when Michael and his wife chose to incorporate my name into Eric's. Just a year or two later, Kevin and his wife gave us our third grandson, Kevin Jarrod Durden Jr.

We had so many blessings and so many healthy, happy grandchildren to dote on. I couldn't help but think about my own mother and how proud she would have been if she could see and visit with her great-grandchildren. Whenever I considered my own children and grandchildren, I always found myself thinking about the life that my mother led. She had experienced so many hardships and she'd had so many challenges arrayed against her, but she had persevered through all of it and she had remained dedicated to her children. It was only as I grew up and went out into the world that I fully realized how instrumental her support had been for my siblings and me. At least in my case, I can't even imagine what my life would have looked like if I hadn't had my mother to lean on.

My mother passed away a very young woman, just a week shy of her fiftieth birthday. I felt as though I had just started to understand her more fully, and then she was gone. As my own children grew into adulthood, however, I felt that I was beginning to understand why she did the things she did for us, the almost-indescribable joy that children bring into their parents' lives. I felt that there was something of my mother in that feeling, that joy and that pride I felt as a father, and I knew I was incredibly lucky to be able to watch as my own sons discovered those feelings with their own children.

While I relished my new role as grandfather, I was still looking for a new career pathway. My answer appeared one day when I came across an article about the benefits of owning an automobile dealership. This could be an exciting venture, I thought to myself. There was one problem, however: I had no idea how to run an automobile dealership.

I couldn't seem to let go of the idea, however. I found myself circling back to it over and over again. Finally, I decided to call the GM (General Motors) headquarters in Simi Valley to request an interview. Within a week's time, I found myself sitting before a GM interviewer, being quizzed about my new interest in car dealerships.

During the interview, they gave me an aptitude test. I hadn't known exactly what to expect from this interview, and I was surprised at the test. I wondered what sort of aptitudes they were looking for. I didn't dwell on the idea, though, because I knew that I had no control over the evaluation of the test. There was no sense in getting disappointed over something that was completely out of my hands.

I never did find out what that aptitude test was designed to measure, but about a week after my visit, I received a phone call from the local district manager letting me know that my finances were in order, my background and education had been checked out, and they could start making arrangements immediately for my entrance into the General Motors Academy.

At that point, the district manager paused for a moment and asked, as though it had just occurred to him, "Would you be interested in attending the academy?"

The academy was, I knew, a dedicated training program that would teach prospective dealership-owners everything they needed to successfully operate their own dealership. It was the next step towards buying and running a dealership. I paused a moment before answering, considering this decision. I still didn't know anything about operating a car dealership, but in theory, this course would give me that knowledge. If I committed to this, I would be committing to an entirely new career trajectory.

"Yes," I said finally, "I think so."

The academy was located in Detroit, the historic home of GM. The company arranged for a rental car and a hotel stay while I completed the course. Not too long after I arrived in Detroit, I got word that the Oakland Raiders had hired Art Shell as their head coach. Art Shell was a former player with the Raiders who had been coaching on the team for the last few years. Now he had become the first Black head coach in modern football. Fritz Pollard had technically been the first in the early 1920s.

This news was surprising, to say the least. Art was a younger coach, though he had been with the Raiders for most of his career. I had always thought that when a Black head coach was chosen, he would probably be selected by someone like Al Davis. Al Davis was the commissioner of the AFL (American Football League), a competitor to the National Football League before the two merged in 1970. He was well-known for hiring people of color and women for pivotal roles in the organizations he worked with.

When the two leagues merged, there was a vote by the owners on which of the two commissioners—Al Davis or Pete Rozelle—would head up the new league (to be called the NFL). Pete Rozelle got the job and, before Al left office, he had named Aaron Wade as an official, one of the few Black officials at that time. He had also famously refused to let his teams play segregated cities in the 1960s.

Considering his track record, it was not exactly surprising to hear of Al Davis's decision—but I was still taken aback. I had thought it would be many more years before an African American rose to the position of head coach. I wondered if Art Rooney II, owner of the Pittsburg Steelers, had been in on the loop. I had met both men, and they both had impressed me as men of great vision who were willing to break with tradition, even if they did so alone.

I immediately sent a telegram to Art Shell to congratulate him on his new appointment. There was, of course, a part of me that couldn't help but wonder what sort of position I would be in now if I hadn't left professional football. At the time, the future had seemed so limited for African-American coaches. With Art's appointment, perhaps things would have been different.

But I didn't have the luxury of spending too much time looking backwards.. I had put all of my efforts—and a great deal of money— into my new venture. I had committed to seeing it through with GM. Besides, I had decided to leave coaching for many reasons, not the least of them my desire to spend more time with my family. I thought owning a dealership would be a great way to bring my sons into a family business. With this in mind, I turned my focus to the GM academy, determined to learn as much as possible from the instructors.

The automobile business is basically made up of five departments: the new car department, the used car department, the service department, the parts department, and the financial department. Any one department by itself can provide an individual with a good, comfortable living. An owner, however, has to figure out how to balance each one of them.

The key is to delegate appropriately. Find good, strong managers and place them in departments where they can thrive. Then, as owner, your job is to manage the managers. To do that, you need to know how each department works. At the academy, we tackled each department, one by one, learning all there was to know about it before moving on to the next. The candidates spent two to three months in the classroom learning conceptually about the business. Then we were each matched with a dealership that had been secured and pre-arranged by GM.

This part of the training was a kind of trial run where we would oversee every element of the business. We had complete freedom over operations at the dealerships while we were there, and we attended all meetings, including district meetings. The idea was to put the candidate in the shoes of the dealer and prepare us to manage our own locations.

The changeover from football to the automobile business did not come easily, and there were some agonizing times. I had to develop many new skills, although some—like evaluating people and placing them in the optimal positions—transferred over from my years as a coach. Overall, I found the automobile business to be exciting and I welcomed the challenge. Perhaps it was the competitive nature that I had developed over the years. We were evaluated on how we performed both in the classrooms and at the dealerships, and I always strove for the highest marks.

After I graduated from the academy, I began looking for dealerships to purchase. The first place General Motors took me was in Oklahoma, in the small town of Bixby, just outside of Tulsa. General Motors had indicated, however, that they were planning to move the dealership into the greater Tulsa area shortly. The facility itself was beautiful and brand new—it was being completed as I visited—but I ultimately decided that it was not for me.

I had changed careers because I'd grown tired of spending so much time away from my family, and I knew I couldn't take on a dealership that was several states away from them. I needed something closer to home. Then GM offered me a dealership in Hayward, California, across the bay from San Francisco. It wasn't a perfect solution—San Diego and San Francisco are practically on opposite ends of the state, after all—but the location seemed viable and the price was reasonable. I accepted. GM had also told me that, if I agreed to take the dealership, they would move it into an even better location—and I knew that, just as in real estate, the name of the game was location.

GM originally had said that they would move the dealership in a year. Three years came and went, however, and I was still in the same place. Around that time, local unions were also making their presence known. They were looking to unionize my service department, and I was resistant, because I knew it would create a significant strain on my bottom line. I could only hold out for so long, however, and I soon had to factor in those extra costs.

Shortly thereafter, GM came to me and apologized for not having moved the dealership as promised. They offered me a new deal. They would help me sell my existing dealership and would relocate me to the Southern California area, which was where I really wanted to be.

It seemed that I would finally have the convenient business that I wanted, with my family on-board. My sons, Michael and Allan, had joined me at the dealership by this time. Michael worked with the sales managers and Allan worked with the service department. Kevin hadn't shown much interest yet, but I was still hopeful he would want to get involved, especially if we moved to a location nearer to Southern California.

Eventually, GM asked me to look at a dealership in Culver City in the Fox Hills Mall area, an upscale part of Los Angeles. It was a good location, although it was about 125 miles away from my home in San Diego.

I felt comfortable with the Culver City location because it wasn't too far from where I'd grown up. I felt that I knew the area and understood the clientele. The vehicle makeup of the dealership was Buick, Pontiac, and GMC trucks, which I felt were a good fit for the area. Even though it wasn't ideal, I decided to take the location. In turn, GM promised to move me even closer to San Diego in the future.

I took over the dealership in 1996 and, by this time, Michael had found another job that he wanted to pursue. I never succeeded in convincing Kevin to come aboard, but Allan made the move with me, becoming my service manager. I felt I was making progress, getting closer to the ideal San Diego dealership and working with my family. What I didn't know—and couldn't have known—was that tragedy was on the horizon.

On the morning of May 26, 1998, disaster struck the Durden family. The day began normally enough. I was about to complete my usual drive from San Diego to Culver City, and I was about half a block away from the dealership when I received a phone call from June. I could hear the strain in her voice as she asked me where I was. I told her that I was just about to pull into the dealership, and she waited while I parked the car before turning my attention back to her.

She told me that Kevin, our middle son, had been stabbed and that he had passed.

I couldn't believe what I was hearing, so I asked her to repeat herself. I listened, but I still couldn't process what she was telling me. For about four seconds, everything went black and I completely lost control of everything, my body and my mind.

When I finally regained my composure, I went into the dealership and found my general sales manager, asking him to please take over and explaining why I needed to return to San Diego immediately.

Word spread quickly through the dealership, and by the time I was preparing to get back into my car and drive those 125 miles back to my grieving wife and the terrible new hole in our lives, one of my employees ran up to me and caught my arm. "Mr. Durden," he said, "we can't let you drive back to San Diego like this. I'll drive you home." To this day, I am so grateful for this act of kindness.

I don't remember much about that long drive, but I know that when I got home, June met me at the door and began to give me all of the details, as much as she knew. There wasn't much to tell. It seemed that Kevin had been arguing with a young man over a cell phone. The young man, as it turned out, was a sixteen-year-old member of the Crips gang who was trying to pick a fight with Kevin. Later, he would admit in court that he had indeed stolen the cell phone that kicked off the argument.

This was the hardest challenge my family had ever faced. It was so hard to even get our heads around the new reality of our lives. We hadn't had any time to prepare for the loss of Kevin; instead, he had been ripped from us with no warning. It had all happened in moments; our son was there and then he was gone, all over a minor disagreement with a stranger.

There was no roadmap for dealing with this kind of tragedy and, to be honest, we had no idea how to handle it. To this day, I'm not exactly sure how we did. Much of that time is a dark blur to me. I remember that June regularly cried herself to sleep and that we leaned heavily upon our faith to get us through.

It felt like the kind of pain that we could not endure—but somehow, we did. Somehow, the world did not stop when Kevin passed. We still had other children and grandchildren, jobs and responsibilities. We had to engage with the world, even though we wanted nothing but to retreat and nurse our wounds. Time passed slowly, and so did the hurting.

In 1999, GM told me that they had found the type of dealership I was looking for in San Diego. I was pleased because, with the loss of Kevin, I was more eager than ever to stay close to my home and family. GM told me they were close to completing a deal and would have a location for me soon, so I put my Culver City dealership up for sale and, in June of 2000, it sold. I moved back to San Diego, where GM promptly informed me that they had run into some unexpected problems and the deal had fallen through.

I'd sold my dealership, so the money could be transferrable—but as the deal was no longer possible, I questioned whether it was in my best interest to keep looking. I decided to look for a deal on my own and quickly discovered that the good dealerships were not for sale.

I took this information to General Motors and they decided to settle with me. The settlement was a cash deal that would put me in the position of not needing to find another dealership. Financially, my family would be in excellent shape. I put some of my money into real estate, an enterprise that I could watch from afar without having to oversee on a daily basis, and that is where most of my interests lie these days. Growing up in a family where we often struggled with money, I am very thankful to the Father that we do not have any financial problems and that June and I have always been able to provide for our family.

I thought then that I had finally reached a point when I was ready to leave the working world, or at least to wind down my direct participation. I wanted to devote time to my children and grandchildren and enjoying myself.

After seven years of marriage, Michael and his wife sadly decided to divorce. This was obviously not an ideal outcome for a marriage, but Michael and his wife were able to maintain a positive relationship and care for their children. Eric and Lisa never wanted for anything, and they definitely knew that both of their parents loved them tremendously.

Michael was single for several years before he met a young lady and decided that she was the one for him. They forged a great relationship, and it wasn't long before they decided to get married. June and I were so happy to see Michael settled down with a wonderful partner.

Michael volunteered as a Little League coach and, one day, he came home from practice feeling unusually tired. He also had a high fever. His new wife, Donna, decided that he should see a doctor, so she loaded him into the family car and drove him to the hospital.

Donna called right away to let us know that Michael was in the hospital, but she said that he was stable and his situation was not considered an emergency. The next day, we drove to the hospital to check in on him. Michael was in good spirits when we arrived, and everyone felt sure that he would be coming home soon. We told him that we would come by to visit him the next day, but he shook his head, saying, "Oh, I'll be back home by then."

It was November 26, 2007. Allan had made arrangements to meet up with Michael that night to watch the Monday night football game, something they usually did together. Instead, Allan called me and told me that Michael had taken a sudden turn for the worse and we should come to Los Angeles at once.

June and I left San Diego immediately and we practically flew the 100-plus miles to LA—but by the time we got to the hospital, Michael had already passed. Eight years before, we had lost one son in the blink of an eye. Now, another blink, another son. How could this be happening to us again?

The doctors told us that Michael had developed blood clots in his lungs, but we couldn't believe what we were hearing. We had seen him just the day before, and he had been cheerful and normal. Could something really have been going terribly wrong inside his body, even as he talked with us and planned for the future?

It seemed too unfair to be real. Everyone expects certain kinds of losses and tragedies in their lives. When my mother passed, I was deeply sad, but I understood that most people will experience the loss of their parents in the life. A parent, however, does not expect to lose their child. To suffer that experience twice seemed so incredibly cruel.

This was one of the lowest points of our lives. My first thought was that I would not be able to survive this additional heartbreak. I knew that I had to find some way to keep going, but I just didn't know how I would. I sat there in the hospital for a long time, searching for something to hold on to, something to keep me afloat in what felt like an endless sadness.

I thought back over my sons' lives and their achievements, the incredible pride I felt for them and the delight they had brought into my life. They had, in many ways, made my life worth living. Now I had to find a way to go on without Kevin and Michael. I prayed for the strength to continue.

Once again, I took solace in the people around me who were alive and important and needed their husband, father, and grandfather in their lives. At first, I had to force myself to continue on for those people that I loved. But as time passed, I began to rediscover some of the joy of seeing my family grow and develop. Though we have had some terrible lows, I could not deny that we had also experienced incredible highs. I have lived a fantastic life with a beautiful family at my side, and I personally have so much to be thankful for.

A simple "thank you" doesn't even begin to cover how I feel about the contributions that June and Michael and Kevin and Allan made to our lives together. I am so grateful to them for all the joy they've brought me all these years.

Allan is my last living child, and I could not ask for a more terrific son. As we dealt with the loss of our sons, he also had to cope with the loss of his beloved brothers while still trying to help us with our grief. He has been an unfailing source of love and support.

We have been blessed with five grandchildren who are now growing into incredible adults. Ryan, our eldest grandchild, is married to Annette Kinslow and they have three beautiful children: Isaiah Kevin Durden, Alyiah Anne Durden, and Sophiah Cali Durden. Eric, Michael's oldest son, now has two children of his own with his partner Ashley Mickens: Maya June Durden (and we thank them for including my wife June's name in Maya's) and Madden Michael Durden. My two granddaughters, Lisa and Alexis, are still in college. Lisa is even working toward her master's degree. I am so proud of all of my grandchildren and great-grandchildren, each of whom is ready to carry on the Durden legacy.

I've had an unusual and often difficult life. I've known loss as well as success. But when I look back on all my achievements, I find myself thinking of my wife and children, my grandchildren, and great-grandchildren. With a family like this, how can I be anything but a winner?

ACKNOWLEDGMENTS

hope that all who read this book enjoy its contents and come away knowing a little bit more about how me and my family have evolved over the years to become the people we are today. The highs and lows of our lives have been harrowing and rewarding and they have given us strength beyond what I can put down on paper.

The limitations of any book mean that, unfortunately, there are always going to be details and elements that don't make it into the final draft. I wanted to take this space to acknowledge some family members who played important roles both in my life and in bringing this book to fruition. The larger Durden family has been an amazing source of love and support over the years, and I want to personally thank my family for their efforts.

My older brother, Nathaniel Durden, had eight children. His youngest, LaShawn Durden Hibbert, a beautiful young lady and a beloved niece, has been invaluable in terms of coordinating our (very large!) family tree. Her siblings include Charlotte Durden, Cheryl Renee Durden, Marlow Durden, Rudy Durden, Victor Durden, Merrill Durden and, finally, the two youngest, LaShawn herself and O-Donu.

I would further like to acknowledge Greg Durden, the only son of my youngest brother, Sammy Joe Durden. My sister, Virginia Nell Durden Hairston, has two sons and one daughter: Darryl L. Lewis, Richard (Bones) Hairston, and LaVialle Lewis. Darryl has two young sons himself: Justin J. Lewis and Darryl L. Lewis Jr. LaVialle has two sons as well, William F. Robinson III and Vernel M. Goff, as well as her daughter, Chanaile L. Goff. Virginia's youngest son, Richard, has one daughter, Ananza L. Hairston. And, my wonderful daughter-in-law, Angela Durden. Of course, I would also like to acknowledge my youngest sister, Condicia Renee Dumas. I would like to offer a special acknowledgement to Sheryl Durden. She is not my biological daughter, but I could not love her any more if she we were.

I'd also like to acknowledge my nieces and nephews on June's side of the family:

Kimberly Oliver Vacha, Carmen Oliver Perez, Carol Ann Pecot, Charles E. Pecot, Justin Pecot Jr., Anthony and Christopher Pecot. I would also like to mention Joseph E. Pecot Jr., Jeffrey Pecot, my godson, and Matthew Pecot, the PhD in the family. My best wishes go out to Joseph Pecot Sr., as well as Alwilda, Samuel, Patricia, and Theodore Pecot.

I wish all of these young people on both sides of the family all of the success in the world.

Last but certainly not least, I would like to recognize the future of my immediate family and the heirs who will carry on the Durden name and legacy, my wonderful great-grandchildren: Isaiah Kevin Durden, Alyiah Anne Durden, Maya June Durden, Sophiah Cali Durden, and Madden Michael Durden.

I love you all and God bless each and every one of you.

DURDEN PHOTOS

The Durden Family. From L to R: Michael, Eric, Earnel, June, Alexis, Allan, Angela, Ryan

Durden Family 2013: Top row – Eric, Alexis, Angela, Allan, Ryan. Middle row – Ashley, Earnel, June, Annett. Bottom row – Amaya, Isaiah, Jayden, Alyiah

New Year's Eve – 2010, Long Beach, CA

Earnel Durden is the second from the left in the top row

Earnel Durden enjoying a vacation in 2014 to Sydney, Nova Scotia

My son, Kevin, age 10, playing for Harbor City, the Jr. Falcons

My son, Allan, at the University of Arizona in 1985
(All American Defensive Back)

Newspaper feature on my grandson, Ryan

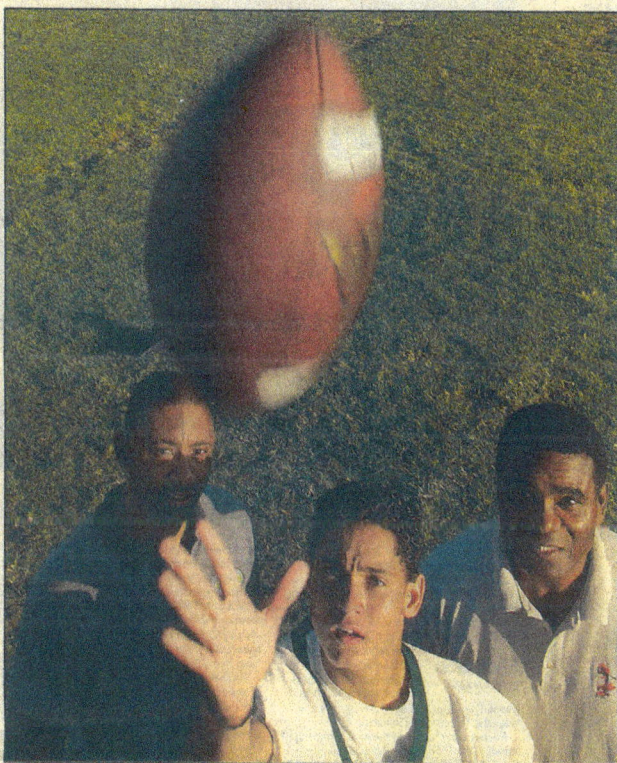

Helix High senior quarterback Ryan Durden is supported by father Allan Durden (left), who played football at Arizona, and his grandfather, Earnel Durden (right), who played at Oregon State. *Jim Baird / Union-Tribune*

New chapter

Latest in Durden line is carving his own niche at Helix

By Bill Dickens
STAFF WRITER

The wall-sized display case inside the La Mesa home of Earnel and June Durden is crammed with trophies, plaques, pictures, programs and memorabilia that trace the family's athletic achievement. Sort of a half-century timeline measuring the blue-ribbon talents of three generations.

Earnel Durden kicked off the family's rich athletic heritage by being named Los Angeles high school football Player of the Year at Manual Arts High in 1954.

"I've played or coached football almost all of my adult life," said Durden, an All-America wingback at Oregon State who played in the 1957 Rose Bowl and spent 13 seasons as an assistant coach for the Chargers. He's also coached with the Rams, Houston Oilers, UCLA, Long Beach State, Compton JC and Compton

High.

And he still isn't finished. The 66-year-old Durden spends much of his time mentoring grandson Ryan Durden — senior quarterback for the Helix Highlanders.

"My dad is excited to have another chance to work with one of his own," said Allan Durden, Ryan's father and the youngest of Earnel's three sons. He's more involved with Ryan's development because he's retired."

Ryan (5-foot-10, 160 pounds) made his first varsity start in Helix's 19-10 victory over Vista last week. Although his individual statistics weren't spectacular, his leadership was sound.

"Until these last two years, I don't think football was that important to Ryan even though he'd been playing it since Pop Warner," Earnel said. "He played just to go along with the crowd, his friends. But now, I think

Durden family tree

A half-century of football accolades:

● **FIRST GENERATION**
Earnel: High school Player of the Year in L.A. Played in 1957 Rose Bowl for Oregon State. Spent 13 years as assistant coach for Chargers.

● **SECOND GENERATION**
Michael: Played at Helix, where he also competed in basketball, track. Defensive back for UCLA. Spent three seasons with Edmonton of CFL.

Kevin: Captain of Helix squad, earning football scholarship to Idaho State. Now deceased.

Allan: Played for 1980 Helix team that went undefeated. An All-American at Arizona his senior season.

● **THIRD GENERATION**
Ryan: Son of Allan. Starting quarterback for Helix team ranked No.

The Durden home in La Mesa